A McL JENKINS

CAST OF A LIFETIME

First published in Great Britain in 2008
by Eccleston Publishing
Spitalhaugh House
West Linton EH46 7BH
sandyjenkins37@tiscali.co.uk

Printed by Meigle Colour Printers Ltd
sales@meigleprint.co.uk

Cover and maps designed by
Nial Smith Design
nial@nialsmith.co.uk

ISBN 978-0-9560980-0-9

Catalogue record for this book is available from the British Library

CONTENTS

DEDICATION

For my wife Pat and for Mark, Andrew and Katharine

ACKNOWLEDGEMENTS

I am immensely grateful to the many companions who have travelled and fished with me on lochs and rivers in various parts of the world as it has been their company which has so enhanced the pleasure of it all. My old friend, David Kilpatrick, in particular encouraged me to write 'Cast of a Lifetime' and for fifty years has been a patient and long-suffering fishing companion. He also provided some of the photographs.

I am grateful to the late Carlotta Astley-Nicholson who showed unbounded kindness to me when I was a child and to the family when we were invited to stay each summer at Arisaig House. She introduced me to the world of Highland burns and hill lochs.

I also owe my parents much for having taught me, as a child, love of nature and for providing me with a bamboo cane and a bent pin with which I persecuted trout among the hills of Moffat so long ago.

Lastly, and most importantly, I must thank my family. My wife, Pat, put up uncomplainingly with my absences during the rather numerous fishing trips and Katharine and Andrew patiently resolved many computer glitches which occurred during preparation of the manuscript.

INTRODUCTION

There are many books about fishing, but catching a fish in one river is rather like catching one in another. It is often other factors which make the pastime so absorbing, including the vagaries of travel in remote regions, contact with indigenous peoples and, not least, the beauty and natural history of what is often a strange environment.

This book encompasses a lifetime of fishing - my own - beginning in boyhood with trout and mackerel and continuing on through years devoted to travel in pursuit of salmon or related species. A child's wide eyed fascination with the world of burns, rivers and lochs at home is described in the early pages while, with growing maturity, the urge to travel with a rod leads to expeditions to the far-flung regions of Iceland, Finnmark in Northern Norway, Finland, Newfoundland, Baffin Island and the Canadian Arctic, Alaska, Northern Russia and Africa. In some chapters, the element of travel and adventure is as prominent as the fishing itself, as described in the Eskimo seal hunt in the pack-ice off Baffin Island. However, the beauty of some of Scotland's own rivers and lochs is not ignored including the melancholy magic of Grimersta in the Outer Hebrides and the bracing starkness of the River Thurso in Caithness.

The book, compiled with the help of my original diaries, is introduced by a letter to my friend and fishing companion, David Kilpatrick. For half a century we have shared the joys of fishing, travel and adventure and without his, and later the company of others as well, the pleasure of it all would have been greatly diminished.

West Linton
8th July, 2008

Dear David,

Sometimes, especially in the dark evenings, my thoughts wander happily among the wonderful fishing experiences which we have shared over the past half century. It is a bit self-indulgent to write about them but it helps me to live through them all over again bringing back the sound of the rivers and the wildness of the hills of our playgrounds of so long ago. No doubt this is just a sign of an addling old brain, but it is fun.

I was looking through some old photographs the other day and came upon a black and white picture, already slightly sepia coloured, of a lonely farmhouse set in a huge Icelandic landscape of fjord and barren hills. Through the millennia a mountain torrent has carried down alluvial deposit which projects like a fan into the fjord and on this one piece of grassy ground stands the farmhouse, 'our' farmhouse, and our river, the Krossa, was only two or three miles away. Of all the rivers and countries where we have fished I know that this desolate spot holds a special place in our affections. The farmhouse on the shores of the bleak fjord was always a haven of warmth and welcome which, in the evenings, revived us after our daily floundering up and down and often in the river a few miles away.

It is difficult to believe that fifty years have passed since we fished together in that remote corner of Iceland, but the memory of the entrancing landscape with its wild rivers and rocky hills is as clear as ever in my mind.

Rivers come in all shapes and sizes, but ours was a little river of real character. I know that you were often drawn miles into the hills to its source from a small lake or 'vatn' where fat trout told of good feeding of some obscure kind. A more lonely spot it would be difficult to imagine. I, on the other hand, was attracted to the mouth of the river where it flowed over the beach shingle to mingle with the sea. The salt smell and steady swish of sea waves meeting the fresh flow was disturbed by shrieking of indignant terns which had young among the salt-bleached pebbles. One really had to hold onto one's hat the birds were so aggressive.

Do you remember what we called, without much originality, the Sea Pool? I was always fascinated by this place and my first stealthy examination over a little rock cliff to the pool below revealed a wonder-world of rocks, clear water and fish - many fish. Some Icelandic rivers are extraordinarily clear and that pool certainly was. Looking vertically down I could see ranks of sea-fresh salmon not ten feet away. Their grey-green forms seemed to hang in air such was the water clarity and beneath them the round sea stones were draped with green and brown strands of wrack. If the salmon had been the only inhabitants of that pool the marvel would have been sufficient, but among them hovered what were, to me, the most unexpected and beautiful fish that I had ever seen. They were smaller than the salmon; greenish backs and silver flanks suffused with a spotted pink sheen set off by white-edged pelvic fins. This was my first sight of that most beautiful fish, the migratory arctic char.

For some time I lay mesmerised by the beauty of this silent water-world in which fish and wrack swayed with a gentle rhythmic pulse of their own. However, as we both now know, an incautious movement, even when lying down, can clear an Icelandic pool of all fish. Leaning forward to get a better view did it. Fish flashed off in all directions and the pool's tail-glide bulged as salmon and char raced for the security of the fjord twenty yards away. Then - not a fish to be seen - just an empty pool with what looked like clear air flowing to the sea and a coloured image which has stuck in my mind for all of fifty years.

Our subsequent expeditions to North Norway and to the Canadian Arctic produced yet more extraordinary travel and fishing experiences and more fun than we could possibly have hoped for. After you were married you were obviously less able to disappear for prolonged periods, so sadly you could not join me on some of the jaunts of later years, but I have written about these all the same and you can skip those chapters if you wish. You may also be excused from reading about my childhood fishy encounters which began away back in the Second World War!

Yours ever

Sandy

Chapter 1

The Early Years

Wartime. The First Glimpse of a Salmon.

In 1940 when Hitler was rampaging through Europe I was three years old. My parents, my brother and I lived on the edge of Wentworth golf course in Surrey surrounded by pine woods and heath which was a wonderful environment for children. However, the peace of those surroundings came to an end when the air raids began. For some reason the German bombers seemed to target the heath itself, perhaps attracted by decoy fires and numerous bombs exploded uncomfortably close to our house. My father roofed over the empty garden swimming pool with heavy timbers which he covered with a mound of earth and, apparently much to my excitement, we spent bombing nights in candle light underground. Sometimes, when the bombs were close, soil sifted down between the timbers onto our heads as explosions shook the earth. My parents tried to amuse us in the candle light by casting shadows of strange animals with their hands onto the walls of the swimming pool. Although my brother and I thought it was all great fun, it was too much for our devoted parents and my mother took us to Scotland while my father stayed to continue war work. A short time in a cottage at Calgary on the Island of Mull was followed by blissful years among the rolling hills and rivers of Moffat in the Scottish border country. To this day I love that countryside and still see my old haunts with a child's eye. It was there that I saw my first salmon.

I must have been five years old when, one day, my nanny fetched my balloon-tyred bike and, wobblingly, we rode out of our

The Moffat Water emerging from the Dumfriesshire hills.

house on Ballplay Road on the edge of Moffat, past the field where soldiers from the barracks practiced bayoneting suspended sandbags in the absence of convenient Germans and up towards the hills where the Moffat Water emerges, sparkling and pure. There a small side road leads to a stone bridge arching over the river, which itself is not more than ten paces across. Ash trees, oaks and alders lean over the water and downstream a green meadow is bordered by the river on one side and by a narrow road, with homely weeds growing up its middle, on the other. Two or three magnificent chestnut and lime trees, neatly cropped up to where grazing cattle can reach, throw patches of deep shade onto the grass.

That day, peering on tiptoe over the parapet of the bridge, my chin resting on the stonework, I saw them. In the lightly peat-stained water, side by side, lay two mysterious long shapes, their backs greeny-

The bridge over the Moffat Water from which in 1942, aged 5, I saw my first salmon.

brown and tails gently moving in the current. I had never imagined that such enormous fish could live in the river that I knew so well and where I had played and swum so often.

In spite of the passing years that scene from the bridge of river and meadow with the shadowy salmon below is one of my abiding memories of those war years, along with bicycle rides on deserted roads, the thump of exploding mortar bombs in the surrounding hills, gas mask practice sessions, pickled eggs in a bucket under the sink and the pianist, Myra Hess, on the wireless playing Bach's 'Jesu, Joy of Man's Desiring.' It is difficult to justify nostalgia for a time when so many were suffering but I feel it just the same.

Once the war was over we returned to Surrey. The house was intact and the surrounding bomb craters had filled with water in which tadpoles were taking up residence. Each summer thereafter we stayed with a friend in a glorious part of the West Highlands near Arisaig which provided ample fishing opportunities.

The Falls Pool which Enchanted a Small Boy.

High in the Arisaig hills in the West Highlands, Borrodale Burn arises from one of many lochans. Far below, the rocky slopes merge into woods and meadows, while in the distance the sea loch stretches towards Ardnamurchan and the Island of Eigg. On the heights, where summer deer graze, the burn is little more than a trickle but it quickly grows as it feels its way in fits and starts down the steep hillside, sometimes in the open and sometimes in deep gullies thick with ferns and mosses. When at last it leaves the hill it is a torrent and races into a deep wooded ravine before plunging into a big pool below. This is a dim, tree-shaded place which, during a spate, is filled with the thunder of the falls and a mist of spray. Water droplets gathering on overhanging ferns, mosses and dark liverworts drip into the pool. Alders arch overhead shutting out much of the sunlight and the steep encircling slopes are covered with russet leaves cast from an enormous overhanging beech tree. On bright days sloping sunbeams pierce the leafy canopy and lance through the peaty water below turning the pool to amber and lighting the gravel bed with a soft orange glow. Then, tiny trout can be seen against the stones, flashing gold as they dart to the surface to pick up some fallen insect. However, even on sunny days not all of the pool's secrets are revealed and, just below the waterfall, to a child it remains a mysterious and forbidding place, deep, dark and filled with swirls and bubbles. On overcast days it even has a hint of menace - who can tell what lives there? Perhaps such places as this gave rise to the old Highland legend of the water kelpie, a horse-like being, which lives in deep pools and must never be touched by a human hand.

One rainy day, many years ago, a small boy scrambled through the wet waterside bushes towards the falls with a rod and a jar of worms. Beneath the beech tree he followed a path leading down the steep slope to the shadowy dimness of the pool. It was a dangerous path, little more than a ledge, with an almost sheer drop of thirty feet to the water below and he was careful not to trip and never looked down. There had been heavy rain the day before and a monstrous surge of water was coming over the falls, far more than he had ever seen before and clumps of golden brown froth with leaves and twigs circled endlessly, round and round, at the pool's edge.

Already, at his age, the boy had learned to keep out of sight of the trout and, once at the pool-side amid the thunder of the waterfall and a mist of spray, he crouched on the stones, unscrewed the lid of the jar and impaled a lively worm on the hook. The worm sank into an eddy beneath the froth and, almost at once, was taken by a little trout which was hoisted out onto the stones. Sometimes grey eels took the worm and they too were lifted, writhing in slimy slip knots, onto the beach. They were a nuisance as they always swallowed the hook and smeared the trace with slime. However, after half an hour the boy had five or six pretty trout to take home. He loved their red spotted golden flanks and, although it seemed a shame to keep them, they were good to eat for breakfast.

As that day wore on and evening approached, the boy's spray dampened clothes struck a chill into his body and he began to feel oddly uneasy beside the thundering waters. He had felt it before at this spot, only today it was much worse - he was becoming strangely afraid. Perhaps it was the loneliness of the place, or the frightening noise and power of the water, but only he knew that it was really the awful black 'deep' just below the falls with its ugly surface up-wellings like black, bunched muscles that filled him with a sense of horror. He watched, appalled, as the muscles seemed to flex and grow in front of his eyes until they looked far too big to be mere water currents. He had always been wary of that part of the pool and in the gathering dusk he felt the grip of panic in his throat. He snatched up his things and, with a pounding heart, rushed up the narrow path beneath the beech tree away from the awful presence in that ravine and with relief emerged at a run, out into the familiar world of fields and hills.

The small boy was, of course, myself, more than sixty years ago, at the age of eight or nine. I have described him in the third person since, with the telescope of time, that is how I glimpse my childish self beside that burn. Many years later I took my own children to the pool and there, swimming and using goggles, we peered into the depths. There was no water kelpie after all, not even in the deep beneath the falls, but there were plenty of little trout and undulating eels probed the crevices among the stones on the bottom.

Perhaps other children fish there now and feel the same joys and fears that I felt so long ago.

The Footbridge

Some of my earliest and happiest fishing memories are associated with Borrodale Burn, in spite of the fears which I once had at the falls pool. Lower down, not far from the sea, the burn is far from threatening and was my playground during many summer holidays after the war.

Each summer my parents, my brother and I were invited by a family friend, Carlotta Astley-Nicholson, to stay at Arisaig House which has magnificent views across Loch nan Uamh, the sea loch, to distant Ardnamurchan. My bedroom was at the top floor and from my window I could see a world that was, to me, little short of heaven. Directly opposite, over the walled gardens and across some fields, the burn runs among alder thickets and to the right lies the sea loch, studded with islands. If I craned my neck further to the right I could just see the grey storm-piled shingle of the beach where the fresh water flows into the sea. During spates, when the burn ran high, from the window I could see tossing white wave-heads leaping above the meadow grass between the alders and I knew that once the spate had settled the trout would be on the take.

*The new footbridge over Borrodale Burn where I lost the sea trout when
aged 11 in 1948*

The mouth of Borrodale Burn with Arisaig House in the distance.

When the conditions were right I used to get up early in the morning and, with a jar of worms, trot down to the burn to fish the peat stained eddies. My pride and joy was to bring back to the house a catch of spotted golden trout - each never more than five or six inches long. These would be taken to the kitchen and solemnly served for breakfast. I had my special, secret place where alders, arching over the burn, were festooned with lichen, some like long grey tresses and some growing on the bark of branches like greenish flattened hands. Beneath these trees was an old wooden bridge with rotting planks and one morning after a recent spate, I plopped my worm into a dark tea-coloured eddy beneath the timbers alongside the old stone foundations, hoping for another small trout. Suddenly there was a violent pull like I had never felt before. Something heavy, very heavy, thrashed about on the surface and there was a flash of bright silver. I pulled with all my might as I always did when I had a bite and normally the victim would fly over my head to land somewhere in the grass behind me. Not so this time and with an audible snap the cast parted and the 'huge' silver thing was gone. My hands trembled so much that I could hardly wind in the remains of the line and I ran as fast as I could back to the house to tell the grown-ups.

The fish was most likely a sea trout or just possibly a salmon. Every year afterwards I tried the same spot hoping for another silver 'thing' but without success - until, that is, I returned thirty-eight years later with my wife and two children. I pointed out the spot beneath the then sadly disintegrated bridge and dropped a worm into the same eddy and gave the rod to my wife who had never fished before. Suddenly, as if in a dream, it all happened again - the sudden pull and something silver thrashing on the surface. My wife shouted for me to take the bending rod and this time with experience of the years, I played and landed a beautiful fresh-run sea-trout of just under two pounds.

The memory of this little episode with its span of so many years means more to me than many memories of later and rather grander fishing experiences, perhaps partly because I was so little, but also as there is such special pleasure in catching fish in small rivers or burns. Even now I sometimes I go back to look at that magic eddy beneath the remains of the bridge. The alders are still there and the peaty water still quietens beside the old stonework - and then I wish that I were young again.

The Hill Lochan

When I was a boy one of the great pleasures of our annual holiday at Arisaig was to fish the small hill lochs high above Loch nan Uamh, the sea loch. Sometimes in August the hilltops were shrouded in cloud which made fishing there impossible but when the tops were clear and if a good breeze was blowing, it was worth making the considerable climb. Once I had climbed to a good height, I used to enjoy resting on a rock to look back over the sea loch to the far distant islands of Eigg and Rum. There always seemed to be a great silence on that hillside save for the occasional drone of a passing bumble-bee on its way to some patch of heather. There are many small lochs in those hills but there is one very special one.

I was a young teenager when, with my rod, I first climbed this particular hill and at the top I came upon a quite small lochan which had a narrow, partly weed-choked arm nearest to me, which broadened to a roughly circular body of water at its far end. The main part cannot have been more than seventy yards across, but judging by the steepness of hillside above, it was probably quite deep and there was another larger loch just over a ridge to the west. As I tramped round the water's edge I noticed scores of tiny frogs hopping among the damp grass and heather, but there were no signs of rising fish. Nevertheless I put up my fly rod and put on an Invicta as a tail fly and a Grouse and Claret as a dropper. After an uneventful hour or two of careful fishing I was beginning to wonder if there were any worthwhile fish there, when I was startled to see what appeared to be a really big trout following my fly quite close to the bank. However, in spite of fishing on I saw nothing else and began to doubt what I thought I had seen.

I would like to be able to say that I persisted with the fly another day with ultimate success, but the truth is not quite like that. It seemed to me possible that the fish were cannibals and that other methods were needed and so it was that, a few days later, I again climbed up to the lochan, this time armed with a small spinning rod and a bottle of preserved golden sprats. With one of these rather smelly offerings, I began casting in the weedy arm of the lochan and within ten minutes something big took and I found myself playing a trout that felt more like a small salmon. I was very careful with it and after a time a most beautiful spotted brown trout of extraordinary size was at my feet among the stones at the shore. I lifted him out by the gills and laid him in the heather. He weighed exactly 3lbs. 13 ozs, was a beautiful fat shape and did not look at all like a cannibal.

When I had admired my catch and had reflected on my good luck I continued casting along the weedy shore. Within five minutes, almost unbelievably, another large fish took and this one too played like a salmon. At first it cut through some weeds, but then came out into clearer water, while streamers of weed caught up on the line zig-zagged across the surface as it strove to reach deeper parts. Finally, after quite a struggle, I was able to beach it among some stones and it joined the earlier trout in the heather. It weighed 4lbs. 10 ozs. What a pair!

The following year I again climbed up to the little lochan, cast a sprat in the same place and in due course hooked and landed a superb trout of 5lbs 7ozs. The year after that was my last but it produced the largest brown trout that I have ever caught which weighed no less than 6lbs 4ozs.

I have never discovered why such extraordinary trout were to be found in that small lochan high up in the rocky Inverness-shire hills and I do not think that the tiny burn entering it would have supported spawning fish. Perhaps the multitude of frogs was the source of food. All of the fish had rich pink flesh and were excellent to eat. My two regrets are that I did not persist with the fly and that I did not return most of these beautiful fish to the water which I certainly would do nowadays.

The Sea Loch and Mackerel.

Childhood holidays at Arisaig were always fun whatever the weather. When it was dull and breezy with plenty of recent rainfall we used to fish the burn or climb to the hill lochs for trout. However, during heat waves, when the sun shone out of a cloudless sky and the burn shrank into its stony bed we used to take a rowing boat out onto Loch nan Uamh, the sea loch, where we swam, dived for clams in sandy coves or fished for mackerel. The boat house, fifteen minutes walk from Arisaig House, looks across a sheltered inlet of russet coloured seaweed to the white, rose-tangled walls of Druimindarroch Cottage. It is an attractive spot and the weedy shoreline creaks with the falling tide, exposing the inhabitants; crabs, shellfish, anemones and, if one looks carefully, slippery blennies and gobies in the rock pools. Beyond the inlet the sea-loch breathes and sighs rhythmically like some slumbering beast as the swell swishes through crevices in the rocks of the scattered islands. Sometimes, however, when the wind is high the beast awakes and, not far from the boathouse, waves surge into a deep rock channel, the pressure exploding out of a blow-hole with a booming exhalation and a plume of spray. On calm days, far to the west, the islands of Eigg and Muck seem to hang between blue sky and sea. On this most beautiful of Highland sea lochs my father, brother and I spent many happy hours trolling for mackerel, saithe and lythe with hand-lines festooned with gaudy feathers on silver hooks. Looking back over sixty years all of those days were enjoyable but there was one particular occasion in the 1950s when we were treated to an remarkable display of nature..

The first sign that something was afoot that afternoon was the behaviour of the gulls. Normally they gathered around the islands with the odd one crossing the loch in search of food, but on this particular day they began to group in increasing numbers ahead of us until there was a white vortex of spiralling, shrieking gulls homing down onto a small patch of sea two hundred yards from our boat, a sure sign that mackerel were about. Then another similar group, also in an apparent feeding frenzy, gathered a little further off.

We rowed as quickly as possible to the nearest flock and let out our mackerel lines. With fifty yards still to go we could see that the sea was boiling beneath the whirling birds as they from above and mackerel from below thrashed at some kind of food source - then we were in among them! Immediately both mackerel lines came alive, heaving and jerking in our hands while below us in the clear water the hooked fish flashed patterns of iridescent blue, green and silver as we wound them in. Every hook had a fish, twelve on each line. Once the mackerel were safely in the boat, flipping and jumping on the bottom-boards, the reason for all the activity became clear as hundreds of tiny fish, like pools of quicksilver, began to crowd against the sides of the boat in an apparent attempt to shelter from the onslaught of gulls and mackerel. Other sinister-looking predators were waiting there too and deep below the stern of the boat a number of lazily swimming dogfish seemed to fly slowly through the crystal watery void. They would not take the mackerel lures but we caught several on a small metal devon minnow. However, we soon stopped as writhing, snapping dogfish are far from pleasant in the bottom of a boat.

After a time we tired of catching and throwing back the mackerel which were feeding so voraciously on the tiny fish. Then, barely fifteen yards from our boat, a school of porpoises appeared, their gleaming black backs arching silently above the surface and then they were all around us as they drove back and forth along the edge of the fish shoal, clearly making the most of the feast.

For a time we sat and watched this display of nature in the raw in which everything seemed to be eating everything else, when we were startled and rather alarmed by the appearance of a large black fin a little way off with a second fin apparently following it. This mysterious object cruised along for ten minutes, occasionally showing a length of dark back, then suddenly it lunged partly out of the water, its huge body raising a sheet of spray as it fell back. At first we thought that it might be some sort of whale, but in hindsight it was almost certainly a large basking shark and what we had assumed to be a second fin was its tail. Our boat suddenly seemed small and fragile in the presence of that monster and, leaving nature to its banquet, we quietly rowed for home.

In the lowering sunshine of that extraordinary late afternoon the gulls were still shrieking in the distance as we rowed back past Cabar Island, its pine trees glowing in the mellow sunlight and later a magnificent sunset fired distant Ardnish Point and the twin summits of Roshven with pink, then purple radiance as the sea loch once again became quiet - save for the sighing of the swell among the islands.

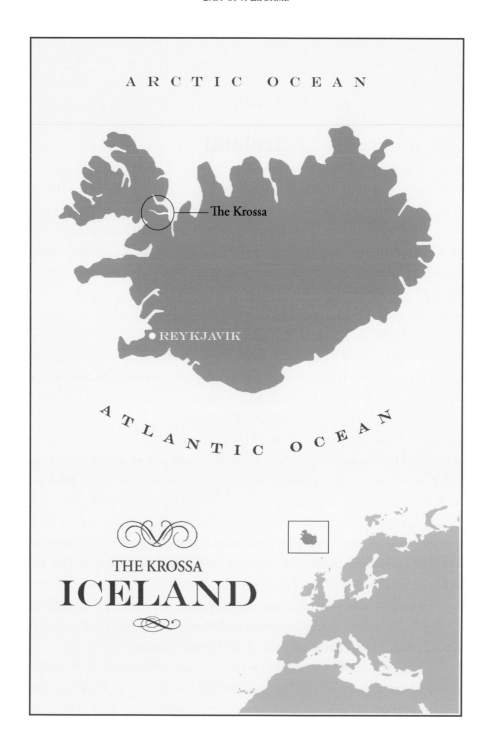

ARCTIC OCEAN

The Krossa

REYKJAVIK

ATLANTIC OCEAN

THE KROSSA
ICELAND

Chapter 2

Iceland

The idea started away back in 1957 in the Cold War years when David Kilpatrick and I, then aged 20, were lounging in deep armchairs in his parent's house in Peeblesshire. One of us suggested going fishing in, of all places, Iceland. The concept may seem ordinary enough nowadays but at that time few people went there and most of our friends thought us crazy. Some seemed to think the place was ice-bound, even with polar bears! The trouble was that it seemed impossible to get information about the fishing. Then, by a stroke of luck, we were advised to go and see Major General R.N. Stewart, a keen salmon fisher, who had an estate in Moidart and a house in Edinburgh. He had written an inspiring book about Icelandic salmon fishing where he was, as far as I can discover, one of the earliest sport fishers. He kindly invited us round to his house in Edinburgh and, after pouring some outsized sherries, enthralled us with tales of Icelandic fishing.

Presently he excused himself and disappeared to make a phone call. On returning he astonished us saying, "I've got Iceland on the phone and there is a river for you. Do you want it?" Did we want it! We most certainly did, and the Krossa in North-West Iceland was ours for a whole summer. To say that we were elated rather understates what we felt. Sometimes life seems to smile on one and it certainly did then. The cost was £100 for the season.

The next few months were joyfully occupied in booking passage on the Icelandic Steamship Company's m.s. Gullfoss, the return trip costing £24 each, and in preparing fishing gear. We even packed an inflatable rubber dinghy, a tent and a set of bagpipes. We were ready for anything!

On July 21st 1958 we boarded the Gullfoss in the Imperial Basin, Leith docks and set sail at 6p.m. straightaway joining a celebration party with some home-bound Icelanders. Next morning in the Pentland Firth it wasn't so funny. A force 7 or 8 gale was blowing. The huge black cliffs of Orkney appeared to starboard with great gouts of white spray breaking at their feet. The wind increased and 20 foot waves surged unbroken over the bows before dissipating in seething masses of foam on the foredeck. With sickening regularity waves swooped beneath the ship lifting the stern so that the propellers heaved above the surface with a rumble of vibration. Standing in the stern enjoying the rhythmic weightlessness as it dropped like a runaway lift did for me and I was felled by appalling seasickness along with many other passengers and several of the crew. It was awful. Thankfully the next day was calmer and gave us time to recover.

The final day dawned bright and calm. The nightmare of the Pentland Firth was replaced by the thrilling sight of the dark and distant coast of Iceland. A glacier and waterfalls gleamed white on the black mountains, but the distance was still too great to make out any details. Then, on a mirror-calm sea, we sailed through the magnificent Westmann Islands where clouds of puffins, guillemots and other seabirds pirouetted among the giant sea-cliffs and stacs, filling the air with their crying and mewing.

Reykjavik turned out then to be a quite a modest little town of low buildings, many with red tin roofs, all sparklingly clean. Disconcertingly the quay beneath our feet, and later the streets, seemed to heave up and down as we transported our bags to a small hotel, a reminder that our centres of balance had not accommodated to terra firma. On resting in a small grassy park in the town several Icelanders furtively sidled up to us in the hope of exchanging their Krona for our Pounds - then not strictly legal but beneficial for both parties. Refreshed by a night's sleep, we set off next morning in a

The farm at Ospakseyri in the north-west of Iceland where David and I
spent a happy summer fishing the Krossa.

tough looking bus with enormously high ground clearance with the baggage securely tied on the roof.

It took no less than five and a half hours on the gravel road to reach Hrutafjördur on Iceland's north coast where we met Steingrimmur Palsson, our Icelandic contact, who drove us the last forty kilometres in his old Russian car. Our destination, Ospakseyri, lay on the north-western 'neck' of Iceland and while it appeared as a substantial dot on the map our farm was the only habitation for miles around. Crouched on a spit of level land projecting into the fjord its sole companion was a neat little red roofed church and some outbuildings. Dark rocky hills rose steeply above it and far off down the fjord a distant headland lay pointing like a finger to the Arctic Ocean. There was not a tree to be seen.

The barrenness of the landscape was more than made up for by the warmth of the welcome from our Icelandic family, Thorkell, his wife Asta and three teenage children. They farmed sheep and had a couple of Icelandic horses. Thorkell, tall, lean and sandy haired seemed to spend a good deal of his time scything hay from not very encouraging patches of wild grass and when resting from his work revived himself by sniffing little heaps of 'neftobak', a kind of coarse snuff, from the back of his hand. His respiratory system seemed to tolerate this, but when we tried it we were driven to paroxysms of sneezing and soon afterwards felt kind of 'high' rather as if we had drunk too many cups of black coffee. Asta, bless her memory, mothered us and on that first evening fed us a delicious dish of smoked mutton. Thereafter it was salmon or char which suited us very well. However, on one occasion which I shudder to recall, she made a special treat of sheep's head, boiled whole, which looked at me reproachfully from my plate with wrinkled eyeballs, blue with boiling which we were encouraged to eat.

We were very contented in the room which we shared. The house was basic by present day standards, having a bathroom and lavatory, but no hot water and there was an electricity generator which was started up for an hour or so last thing in the evening. After that it was candles.

Shortly after arriving we were taken by a three cylinder tractor several miles away to where some horses were grazing and three were caught, one each for us and one for Thorkell. It was late in the evening and the light was poor and to my alarm bridles were provided but no saddles and a headlong gallop ensued along the fjord shore. It was horrifying. It was all I could do to stay aboard and the prospect of my beast stumbling among the many rocks was too awful to contemplate. Amazingly we made it home unscathed and exhilarated. Transport to the river thereafter consisted of these two attractive but often

The author, aged 21, beside the Krossa and the marvellous horse which coped so well with both boggy and rocky terrain.

infuriating horses, one a bay and the other a grey. Fishing in Iceland promised to be entertaining.

The Krossa is a little gem of a river lying in the wildest of landscapes and, apparently, had not previously been sport fished. The lower reaches run through a wide valley clothed with a kind of gravelly tundra dotted with tussocks of beautiful sub-arctic flowers. Further upstream the terrain is grassy with one or two distant farms gleaming against the dark hills and four or five miles from the sea a waterfall or 'foss' blocks the way to migrating fish. Above this the heightening valley broadens into a wide, sweeping boggy moor lit with white heads of bog cotton. Higher still the slope steepens and just under the sky the river source, a mountain lake, is ringed with grim, dark hilltops veiled with drifting cloud. This little lake proved to hold exceptionally fine brown trout and David caught several in the two to three pound range.

There must have been a good food source of some kind to produce such beautiful fish. It was a lonely, gloomy place and silent save for the sigh of the wind and the mournful "mew" of the northern golden plovers. Our horses hated it probably as it was so far from home.

The 'foss' on the Krossa, impassable to salmon in low water, but the two pools below were alive with fish.

As luck would have it our arrival in Iceland coincided with the end of a drought but our first sight of the river was disappointing: little more than a trickle of water ran among the boulders but the rain came during our first night. It rattled on the farmhouse windows and on the corrugated iron roof in a night-long deluge so that, by morning, the hillsides gleamed with countless streams and waterfalls filling the Krossa with a surging flow. White rapids raced into marvellous looking pools and a serious attack of 'fishing fever' overcame me. I could not wait to get started.

I began fishing in the tidal reaches and saw several swirls and one jumping fish. Walking up the river I came upon a very inviting looking pool where I met with David who had moved a good fish further upstream. We came to call this Lunch Pool as we felt sure that it would prove to a focus of our fishing in the weeks to come, but curiously neither of us ever touched a fish there. We settled down to our sandwiches by the pool with a little red-necked phalarope for company which bobbed about the surface picking up invisible morsels. On that first day neither of us caught a fish perhaps because they were busy running in the surge of fresh water. However, in the course of the following weeks we landed forty-two salmon or grilse and many more beautiful arctic char.

As the days passed we settled into an enjoyable routine. Each morning after a breakfast of porridge we had to saddle up our horses. This was no easy task when it came to girthing up as the they blew their bellies out to ensure that they would have comfortably loose corsets for the day, but we usually managed to deflate them and off we would go for the two or three mile canter along the fjord to the river - rods on backs, sandwiches in pockets and hopes high for an exciting day. Flotillas of eider ducks mewing softly on the fjord were replaced near the river mouth by nesting terns, screaming and squawking as they dive-bombed us. I cannot imagine a more wonderful way to start a day's fishing. Before we put up the rods the horses had to be hobbled to prevent them from disappearing into the wilderness by tying their forelegs together with a length of old rope which they seemed to accept with looks of weary resignation and which allowed them to walk a modest distance only, using an odd looking leap with the tied forelegs.

Naturally, some days were more successful than others, but there was one particularly memorable one when I rode the three or four miles to the falls which were then impassable to salmon. Just above these the flow was compressed into a narrow rocky channel leading to the vertical falls below The sheet of water plunged into a gloomy and very deep rock-lined pool which we named the Cauldron, its greenish depths filled with tiny bubbles like an unstoppered lemonade bottle. The thundering falls and the spray made it difficult to see clearly what was going on below, but on this occasion I peered down on my hands and knees and was surprised to catch sight of what seemed to be the tail of an unusually big fish. Then the owner of the tail, a big grey-green form, drifted from under the submerged cliff five feet below me and then sank back out of view again. There was no chance of using a fly in this situation, so I threaded two big lobworms onto my biggest shrimp fly and dropped this hybrid monster into the depths. Almost at once he was on which was quite a problem as I was using my old split cane trout fly rod with 6lb breaking-strain nylon. At first the fish surged around the quite small confines of the pool and then went for depth. An extraordinary amount of line disappeared vertically downwards, but after about twenty minutes he came up and took station in the tail glide. Then, perhaps sensing his mortal danger, he turned abruptly downstream and raced for the sea.

I have never had such a shin-cracking, knee-battering run after a fish in my life. I fell repeatedly among boulders in an effort to keep up and all the time I could see the fish clearly among the rapids still swimming, seemingly unstoppably, downstream. During this chaotic run there was a splintering crack as the top section of the rod broke off and shot down the line, presumably striking the unfortunate fish on the side of the head. A redoubled frenzied burst of speed took the fish another fifty yards downstream until he became stranded in shallows at the edge of some rapids allowing me to grab him above the tail and drag him clear of the water. He was a good cock fish of fifteen pounds, had taken me an hour to land and had run two hundred yards down from where he was hooked. He was the biggest fish that we caught in Iceland and I hardly noticed my bruised and lacerated shins in that moment of triumph. The rod top section was retrieved and was taped back on to provide a rather odd-looking but useable weapon.

The behaviour of this fish was typical of many others which we played and although they might at first stay in the pool where they were hooked most made a dash downstream when they felt that things were getting desperate. I had not been aware of such a consistent pattern of behaviour before and it is tempting to think that the fish were instinctively trying to reach the security of the sea.

It might be asked why we used such light rods and tackle, but most of the fish were in the six to ten pound range and the river itself was relatively tiny. As well as this the many arctic char which we caught were only around the three-quarter to two pound range and, on our rods, were great fun to catch. These colourful fish took freely almost any pattern of fly and we returned most of them, just keeping the odd one for supper. Their flesh was very pink and, I think, tasted even better than that of a salmon.

Although the char took any fly we soon found that the salmon also took any pattern - so long as it had a piece of earthworm attached! We quickly discovered that clear-water worming for salmon in a small river is an art form in itself and perhaps demands of more skill than does fly fishing. It was essential to keep out of sight as even a rod tip over a pool spooked the fish. Our usual method was to stalk a pool at the crawl and to fish more or less lying on our stomachs. The worm had to trundle along in the current unimpeded and if checked or dragged it would be ignored. We also used conventional fly fishing, but in any case I can truthfully say that all our fish were taken on the

*Keeping out of sight of salmon while fishing the second pool below the falls.
Fish on!*

fly even if in many cases it was garnished with a worm! Who is to say
if the fish went for the fly or the wormy part of the contraption? Some
parts of the river were so much more productive than others, but in
the half mile nearest to the sea we never caught a single fish. The
salmon seemed to run straight through this section though we did
catch the odd char there. Many of the middle section pools provided
good sport but the pool thirty yards below the Cauldron was in a
class by itself. It was hotching with fish and it says something for our
conservation instincts that we strictly limited our access to it. One
day, however, we decided to go for it! We dismounted on a marshy
slope nearby where there was some rough grazing for the horses, and
having hobbled them, crept down to the stony beach on our side of
the pool. Opposite, a very steep slope ended in a rock wall which ran
vertically into the water and in this deep part, swept by the main

current, the salmon lay. The pool was really quite small and we decided to take it in turns to fish. Our agreed policy was to hustle a hooked fish downstream out of the pool as quickly as possible in order to minimise disturbance. I began by casting into the run-in and almost immediately a fish took, then raced towards the opposite shore and landed up high and dry on a flat rock where it flapped and thrashed about. Well, this was too good to be true! I jumped into the rapids below the pool and crossed over just in time to see it slither back into the water where it fought for another ten minutes before being landed. It was a beautiful fresh-run fish of ten pounds.

On that day we caught twelve salmon and lost quite a few more before feeling that the fish had been persecuted enough. In those days it was almost unheard of to return salmon to the water but we tucked several under our arms and made wild dashes cross-country to above the falls and deposited them in the virgin waters of upper Krossa. Initially they may have felt surprised and gratified at this, but later perhaps rather frustrated when the scarcity of mates became apparent at spawning time.

We became very popular at the few isolated farms where we distributed fish surplus to our own needs, but carrying them was a problem. I tried tying pairs of fish together leaving a short length of twine between them and slinging them across my horse's back. With half a dozen salmon hanging wetly round its flanks I mounted but was unprepared for the reaction. My usually placid steed bucked me off and I landed face down in the marsh with the wretched animal looking down at me in apparent surprise.

In the middle reaches of the river there was a particular pool where various odd events happened. One day I was fishing some fast water immediately above it when I hooked a very lively salmon which decided to charge down into the deep, clear pool below. To my consternation it had run through a tunnel beneath a large, round boulder and was rushing around in the pool. As the line grated inside the tunnel disaster seemed imminent and I waded into the rapids and tried to pass the rod through the narrow space but the reel kept getting stuck though the fish was still in contact. There was nothing else to do so I sat in the river embracing the boulder and started rocking it. Suddenly the line sprang free and I was back in proper contact. A quick run down to the pool revealed the fish directly below me playing about at the bottom which seemed a very long way down. The pool had sheer underwater rock walls and I was in the unusual situation of playing a fish 'vertically.' Suddenly, to my surprise, a second salmon appeared with its mouth agape and which made repeated lunges at my fish. I could feel jolts coming up the line as the fish struck and this went on for three or four minutes and then the interloper vanished. I hesitate to say that, in spite of all I could do, my fish played for three hours. Perhaps the surge of the inflow to the pool made it impossible to end the struggle more quickly. Thinking that it might be a much bigger fish than it at first appeared, David valiantly ran, as it turned out unnecessarily, a mile or two to fetch a net only to find me landing a nine pound fish when he returned. Understandably his humour was, for a time, in rather short supply.

Another day we found a cormorant on this pool which was annoying as we had especially wanted to fish there. He was obviously so full of fish that he was unable to fly and simply dived when we came close. We decided that he had to be removed and, using large rocks thrown near but not at him, we at last cornered him in a rock crevice. Unwisely I grabbed the unfortunate bird by the neck and he, not unreasonably, bit deeply into one of my fingers. A black, flapping, blood bespattered battle ensued with the creature doing its best to slice up more fingers, but we finally won and rode home with the bird in David's game bag - its head sticking out but with beak tied shut with a handkerchief. Once home we undid the bag, freed his beak and released him on the fjord. A few days later we saw a cormorant flying over the same pool.

There is, of course, so much more to a fishing expedition than just catching fish. Plant, animal and bird life contribute enormously to the overall enjoyment. Many species of flowers grew in colourful clumps on the low-lying ground around the river, including dwarf yellow arctic poppies and saxifrages, while on the higher boggy moor there was an abundance of white bog cotton and several species of orchid. The beautiful northern golden plovers, sometimes with the sun gleaming on the flecked gold of their breasts, flopped along in front of our horses offering themselves in broken-winged sacrifice to draw us away from their young. Once we disturbed a covey of ptarmigan high in the hills and higher still at the lake a pair of whooper swans flew off on our approach.

Iceland is a wonderful country to anyone who is interested in fishing and wildlife and its spell has never quite left us. On the fiftieth anniversary of our time there David and I together revisited the river and the farmhouse where we had stayed so long ago. The old magic was still there. The landscape and the river were quite unchanged, but strangers occupied the farmhouse.

The Icelandic poacher arrested on the Krossa and which bit me.

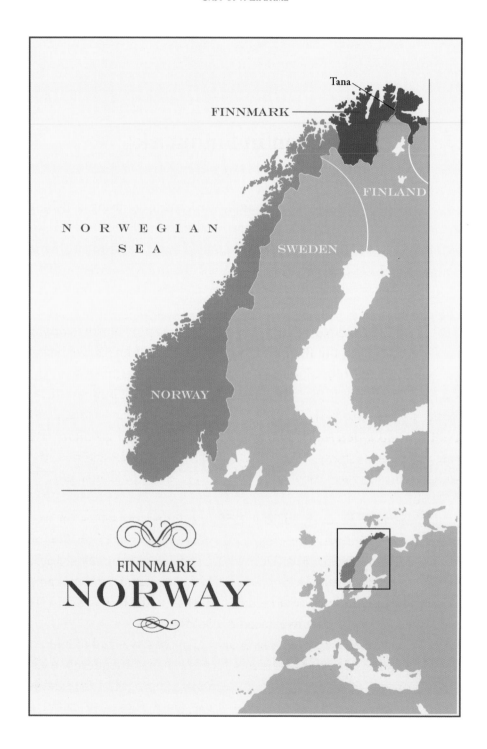

Tana

FINNMARK

FINLAND

NORWEGIAN
SEA

SWEDEN

NORWAY

FINNMARK
NORWAY

Chapter 3

Salmon in Finnmark

In the far off 1950s, dreaming up and organising a fishing expedition was, for me, a major part of the fun of the enterprise. It usually started on some winter's evening when David and I spread out maps of various northern countries and tried to picture rivers with such evocative sounding names as Tana, Laxa or the fabled Alta.

So it happened one day that a large map of North Norway was spread out on the floor and, on our hands and knees, we began to look at the curling blue lines of rivers flowing northwards to the Barents Sea through the intriguingly named area of Finnmark three hundred miles north of the Arctic Circle. Youthful enthusiasm quickly built up into a determination, one way or another, to go there. We knew almost nothing about the salmon fishing possibilities, but judging by the map they had to be good. We would just have to 'freelance'.

Six months later, in July 1959, we found ourselves on m.s. Nordsternan sailing up the length of the Norwegian coast from Bergen with David's little Morris Minor, which had been slung aboard in a net, parked on the foredeck. It was packed with fishing and camping equipment and had two spare wheels attached to the roof which were essential for the rough, unsurfaced Arctic Highway.

The journey up the rocky Norwegian coast was full of interest and, apparently, dangers as the m.s. Nordsternan subsequently went to the bottom! After sailing past the discouraging sight of the rusting remains of a ship wrecked on one of the many rocks, we called at numerous small towns, including Bodo, with its brightly painted houses clustered round the shore. Bodo had been completely rebuilt after its destruction in the Second World War. Then on through the Lofoten Islands, their black peaks streaked with snow, and at Svolvaer a mountain of fish heads on the dockside almost suffocated us with the stench. Sometimes at night we would wake to find ourselves docked at some small harbour with a cluster of locals gossiping round the ship in the northern night-time sunshine. There always seemed to be someone who was appallingly drunk.

At Hammerfest the car was unloaded and the hunt for rivers began. The Arctic Highway presently led us across a beautiful looking river, the Repparselv, crystal clear and very fast flowing. Peering over the bridge we could just make out the shadowy outlines of several salmon. Further on, looking even more attractive, was the Stabburselv and further still the Borselv. Here a lone tent stood near the river and we stopped because, on it, there was a little British Field Sports Society pennant. To our surprise a young German fisher emerged who, in due course, explained that, as a German, he was afraid to be recognised as such in view of the destruction of the area in the War. However, he proved to be very pleasant but had caught no fish. Some days later when we, ourselves, asked an elderly Norwegian lady if we could get something to eat, she studied us suspiciously for a moment and then asked if we were German. This attitude was, perhaps, understandable in view of the scorched earth policy inflicted on northern Norway by the withdrawing Wehrmacht which left barely a building standing in the hope of delaying possible Russian pursuit.

The Stabburselv had looked the most attractive fishing proposition and we retraced our route to the bridge over the river. Having found a rough track up the river's right bank we set off upstream accompanied by a violent thunderstorm. Forked lightening flashed alarmingly close and its ripping, tearing sounds across the sky were followed by enormous booming explosions. The car seemed very exposed on the open tundra and, idiotically, we thought it safer to hide under a groundsheet in a small hollow! After half an hour, very damp but having escaped electrocution, we came to a hut among the riverside pines and beside it was a Norwegian, rain dripping from the brim of his hat, smoking salmon in a barrel. That seemed a good omen and we pitched the tent and fell into conversation. He generously offered to take us upstream in his boat the following day to a good salmon pool below the falls. That night it rained hard and by morning the river looked perfect.

The journey next day was accomplished by means of poling and paddling, but in the rapids we had to get out and pull. Finally some really serious rapids barred the way and we had to abandon ship and walk for half an hour but a marvellous sight then greeted us. Up ahead the falls surged over a rocks and plunged into a wide pool down the middle of which the current continued for a hundred yards until it spilled out and raced down the rapids below. The scent of pines and the birch forest filled the air and now and then the silver arc of a head-and-tailing salmon broke the surface of the pool. It was a beautiful place, and a salmon fisher's dream. In some excitement we put up the rods, mine being an antiquated, heavy 15 foot greenheart affair. In this day of high powered rod technology to have used such a weapon seems extraordinary, but use it I did and later it broke in half during a perfectly normal cast. I selected a medium sized Jock Scott, one of my favourite flies, and began at the neck of the pool while David started at the middle.

Within a few minutes something plucked at the fly - and then again - and a fish took off. The rod made short work of what turned out to be a little grilse of about 3 lbs. There were several more takes but for some reason they became unstuck, probably owing to my then bad habit of tightening on a fish too soon. After an hour a big fish took near the tail of the pool and immediately ripped off 40 or 50 yards of line, jumping several times. To this day I can see that fish, certainly the biggest that I had ever hooked, leaping across the pool. It was on for about five minutes. Then disaster! During our journey one of the rod's rings had been slightly flattened and I knew about this but had ignored it with the result that I deserved. The junction between the line and backing stuck in that ring as the fish made another spectacular run and that was the end. How big was the fish? I shall never know, but my diary says that he must have been about 25 lbs. It is curious how a lost fish is often more memorable than one on the bank and mine, at any rate, are always bigger than any that I land!

It was time for a rest and so we ate the grilse and our Norwegian friend departed in the boat promising to return in a few days. Habitually we carried almost no food with us on fishing trips and relied on catching enough to eat. The problem was that the salmon run seemed to have moved on upstream and apart from a small arctic char - a mere hors d'oeuvres - we caught nothing else. We were listless, hungry and irritable by the time the boat returned to pick us up two days later. In spite of this the Stabburselv is firmly tucked into my memory as one of the most beautiful of rivers and if we had been more experienced I am sure that we would have had a number of fish. In serious need of a wash, a good feed and real beds we pushed on to Lakselv where a small hotel amply provided all of these and gave us time to consider our next strategy.

From several sources we had heard rumours about the huge salmon of the Tana River which forms the northern border between Norway and Finland and we decided to give it a go. This involved a hundred mile drive along a gravel road across open tundra with spectacular views of the arctic coast near North Cape. Sometimes we passed groups of reindeer which gathered in breezy spots to avoid flies. On reaching the Tana and being a bit tired of tent life we found a small guest house in the village of Sirma, quite near the river. It was a simple house in which we shared a room. On arrival we were shown around which included inspection of the lavatory - a shed in the woods in which there was a bench with a row of bottom-sized holes, with an unmentionable black drop below. I cannot remember a latch on the door and the potential for animated conversation with a seated

The lower Tana in Finnmark near the Barents Sea. A 'big fish river.'

neighbour did not appeal and we used to go through the frontier post across the river into Finland when necessity demanded and where reasonable facilities existed. Having settled in we went to inspect the river.

The Tana really is a 'great' river, one or two hundred yards wide, with shores rather than banks. Its powerful flow slides along between shorelines of pale stones and gravel contrasting with bright green birch scrub of the tundra. Now and then the flow picks up as it surges over some underwater ridge, but nothing had prepared me for the sight of the Storfoss, or great rapids. Just above these the current accelerates in a frightening slide and then for three quarters of a mile the river charges in a straight run through a defile in a maelstrom of racing water - black

An albino reindeer by a river near the North Cap of Norway trying to catch a breeze to avoid flies. Jumping salmon showed repeatedly in the river behind.

rocks trailing streamers of white foam far downstream and evil-looking standing waves give warning of the likely fate of any fisherman who might stumble. Far away among the boulders of the opposite shore was the lone figure of a fisherman and at his feet there were two enormous salmon. That did it! The sight of those big fish once again triggered one of my attacks of fishing fever. We hurried back to the guesthouse where our host kindly arranged for a local Saami boatman to take us out that very evening as fishing was best during the light nights. The boatman examined our fly boxes with care and selected several of the largest flies, but curiously, he rejected any that had one of its jungle-cock cheeks missing, indicating that this made them useless.

Waiting at the shore-line was one of the beautiful Tana-pattern boats. Whereas, in Scotland, we are accustomed to fish from fairly

The author above the lower part of the Storfoss on the Tana in 1959.

stout, dumpy dinghies, this was different. It was a low, narrow, elongated craft whose sleek wooden lines swept up at the bow and stern in an echo of its ancient Norse pedigree - a greyhound of a boat, slim and fast and well suited to coping with the strong current. We settled ourselves in and, with the help of a little outboard motor, travelled upstream for fifteen minutes. Then, with the engine stopped, our boatman rowed allowing us to drift slowly downstream while we fished using a mixture of casting and harling. For quite a long time nothing happened, but then David hooked a fish. Far from being a Tana giant this was a little grilse of about 3 lbs. Later I had a similar fish and we pulled over to the Finnish shore where another boat had stopped. Soon a small fire was boiling a black kettle. The fish were cut into two equal sides and birch sticks, which had been peeled flat, were inserted between the skin and the flesh. Then, with a liberal scattering of salt, they were roasted over the fire. The Saami carried brightly

The attractive, slim boats used on the Tana.

patterned leather pouches of ground coffee and I cannot recall a more delicious impromptu picnic under the midnight sun - roast salmon eaten straight off the stick and washed down with strong coffee. I have to admit that the occasional dram of whisky went down as well. The Saami were very friendly but spoke no English though I cannot recall any difficulties in comprehension. One or two of them had quite oriental features and were perhaps descended from some other ethnic group such as the Nentsy who live along the Arctic coasts of Russia. In 1959 the Cold War was at its height and Finland, being in the sphere of influence of Soviet Russia, informal landings on the Finnish shore were forbidden.. This, of course, simply gave an added frisson to such picnics. Later on in the night we caught several more small grilse, but it was not for these that we had come to the Tana.

Two nights later our fortunes changed. We were out in midstream and at about 11 pm. David had a strong take. This, clearly, was no little grilse and the fish made a number of powerful runs taking out about 80 yards of line. Finally it came to the boat, and when it was ready, our Saami boatman produced a curious kind of gaff - a 10 inch wooden handle with a recurved sharp metal spike at one end and with this efficient little weapon he lifted a 21lb. fish cleanly aboard. It was a beautiful deep bodied fresh-run specimen. For fifty years a photograph of this fish with David and the boatman has adorned my fishing album.

David Kilpatrick in 1959 with his 21lb salmon and Per Porsanger our Saami boatman.

David in happy mood after catching his big fish.

Shortly afterwards we resumed fishing. Soon the boat began to gather speed and a hundred yards downstream I caught sight of some rapids. Down we went into them with our lines trailing downstream. The boat bucked about among the waves and our boatman worked hard to keep the bows pointing upstream. Just then I felt a strong pull and the reel let out that wonderful song which indicates a good fish. The trouble was that the song continued and I could do nothing about it as we were swept down the rapids. Then, to my surprise, a good-sized salmon appeared porpoising upstream through the waves not three yards from the boat and I could clearly see my line looping downstream from its mouth. By this time just about all the backing was out and then, to my consternation, bare spool began to show. Disaster seemed imminent as there was nothing left on the spool. To lessen the inevitable shock I threw myself towards the bows but instead of the expected breakage the fish stopped; I was back in contact and was able to regain some line. Fortunately the fish accompanied the boat down the remainder of the rapids and ten minutes later we had him aboard - again a beautiful fish, this time of 18lbs.

These turned out to be our largest salmon from the Tana and although we continued to fish during the next few nights we caught mainly grilse, though these had the advantage of being ideal for our illegal picnics in Finland.

On leaving the Tana we passed through the border control and drove south into Finland through endless forest and past dark, pine-shrouded lakes. Once we found ourselves on a little used track and came to an area of blasted trees where a battle had clearly taken place. Rusting 'scuttle' style steel helmets lay on the ground with one wedged on the dead stump of a pine tree along with the twisted remains of some military vehicle. These were probably fourteen year old relics of the 'Lapland War' when, in 1945, Finnish troops finally expelled the Germans.

Our subsequent explorations took us along the coast towards Tromso where we were to board the m.s. St.Swithun for the journey back to Bergen. On the way another lovely looking river, the Nordriesenelv, caught our attention and once again we were shown great kindness by the locals. A farmer gave us the key to his riverside cabin and allowed us to fish and would accept no payment. The happy result was a perfect 11lb. fish which, on leaving, we presented to our host much to his delight.

Looking back after 50 years, David and I are left with the happiest memories of Norway - a wonderful country with spectacular rivers and some of the kindest people that we have ever met.

Postscript

David and I returned to visit the Tana in 2003, the forty-fifth anniversary of our original trip and happened to stay in a small hotel in the forest on the Finnish side of the river. On hearing of my interest in fishing the proprietor asked me to follow him down to the freezer room. There lay the most magnificent salmon that I have ever seen. It had been caught the previous week on a very small fly in the nearby Tana and weighed no less than 42 lbs.

During this anniversary visit we wondered if any of the Sirma locals would remember some of the people whom we had met when fishing the Tana nearly half a century previously. It was a hot summer and we saw a middle-aged lady resting on the veranda of a small house among the birch trees. We explained who we were and showed her our old photos. Immediately she recognised our two boatmen as her father and her uncle, sadly both now dead. A young girl in one picture turned out to be herself and she even recognised an attractive pony as her own! She was quite overwhelmed with surprise and insisted that we should meet her relatives the next day so that they, too, could see the photographs. A very happy family gathering resulted.

The Tana from the Norwegian side looking across to Finland.

Watched by reindeer on one of the many small rivers near North Cape.

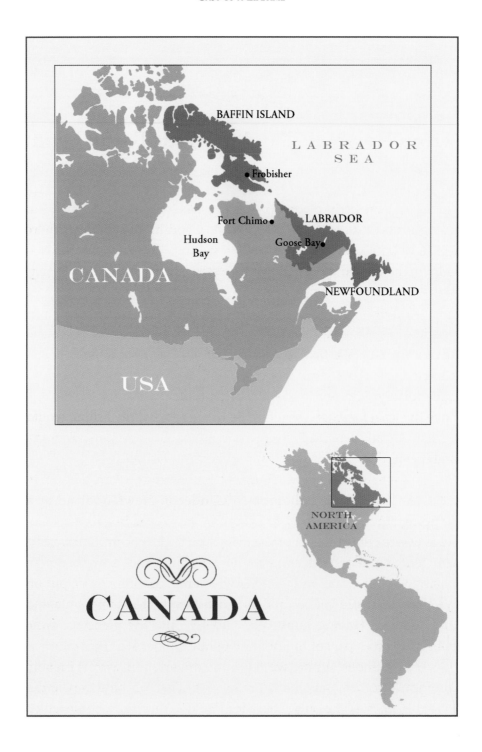

CANADA

Chapter 4

From Newfoundland to Arctic Baffin Land

A fishing trip made up as one goes along is usually great fun though is best suited to the time of one's youth. In later years there seems to be a tiresome need to plan fishing, to know where one is going to sleep and where the next meal is coming from and this gets in the way of a lot of enjoyment.

In 1960, when we were both 23 years of age, David and I decided to go 'freelance fishing' in Canada and we would make no advance plans. We had no real idea of where to head for but were attracted by the Labrador coast which, on our map, looked so outlandishly wild and unspoilt. The problem was that we did not have the least idea how to get to the rivers or what the fishing would be like. A trans-Atlantic flight was the extent of our forward planning and inevitably we were to have problems.

We had arranged to fly from Prestwick airport on July 19th in a B.O.A.C. Britannia turboprop to Gander in Newfoundland as a stepping stone on the way to Labrador. However, in a fore-taste of what was to come the first problem arose at the check-in. Our waders and tent markedly exceeded the weight allowance so rather than paying we unpacked and, watched by bemused airline staff, put on waders and stuffed shoes and as much heavy gear as possible into our pockets. Having lumbered clanking onto the plane we were obliged to cross part of the Atlantic in hot, rubberised discomfort.

At Gander airport we fell into conversation with a friendly American-Scot who said that we really ought to try fishing the Gander River before pushing on to Labrador. He was carrying a bottle which he said contained 'Screech Rum' and I asked him why it was called that. "Because it makes you screech!" he replied and after helping him to drink a fair amount of the contents we found that he was not far wrong. A local bus took us, somewhat inebriated, 20 miles or so to where the road crossed the Gander River where we disembarked. Propelled by rum, we and our kit rolled down an embankment to find ourselves on the bank of a beautiful streamy river running through spruce and birch forest. The small village of Glenwood was not far away and we found a boatman who, for five dollars, agreed to take us downstream to Petrie's Rock - apparently a good fishing spot. Things were looking up.

The canoe trip down-river through numerous gentle rapids and stretches of placid water was most pleasant and an hour or so later we were comfortably camped on an island beside a short stretch of rapids. Our boatman departed promising to return in a few days. It was an idyllic spot. In front of the tent was a small pebble beach and in the warm sunshine the smell of resin wafted from the spruce forest behind us. Encouragingly, one or two small but bright silver grilse showed in the fast water opposite us. We had almost no food supplies with us and our thoughts turned to catching supper.

Without delay we set up our trout fly rods and selected some locally made moose hair flies with stiff black hackles and silver bodies. The edge of the rapids was easy to fish and before long we both caught some beautiful trout-like little fish of up to half a pound which had spotted flanks and red bellies and were known locally as 'mud trout.' These attractive creatures did not deserve such a grubby-sounding name and they were, in fact, char. They made a delicious fry-up and, along with a sea-trout, supper was most satisfactory, even though the char had tapeworms in their intestines.

The grilse continued to show midstream in the rapids and in attempting to reach them I soon fell in. Thereafter I abandoned my water-filled waders and fished in shorts and bare feet, half swimming and half wading. Whilst this was chilly, it gave a great sense of freedom and I was able to put the moose-hair fly just where the fish were showing and soon had two little grilse of three and a half pounds each. On light tackle they were fun to play as they jumped around in the rapids. Clearly we were not going to go hungry.

After a good night's sleep in the tent followed by a fishy breakfast, I noticed that one or two good sized salmon were showing below a flat topped rock which lay in midstream at the lower end of the rapids. That rock looked like a perfect platform for a few casts so I waded into the rapids some fifty yards upstream. The current was quite strong and I was soon off my feet and swimming out to a point where it seemed likely to carry me down to the rock, rod gripped crosswise in my teeth. Suddenly, to my alarm, a canoe, the first that we had seen, powered by an outboard motor appeared upstream but heading straight for me in the rapids. It was coming very fast but luckily just missed me and only at the last moment did the two fishers notice the rather odd sight of a head, rod in mouth, doing an evasive crawl among the waves.

After clambering, dripping, onto the rock, I again saw a good fish moving within easy reach. On my third cast he took, and straightaway made off downstream. I was quite unable to follow as he stripped off more and more line which ultimately snagged round another rock and that was the end of that! Who knows what size he was? He might have been a big one but probably wasn't.

Sadly our boatman returned a day or two early to pick us up as he had to go to fight a huge forest fire and we spent that night on benches in Glenwood station waiting room and in the morning woke under the critical gaze of disgruntled travellers who had nowhere to sit. Then it was back to Gander to catch a plane to Goose Bay in Labrador, but not before we discovered that a grilse which we had left safely in the boat overnight had been eaten by cats. So much for lunch that day.

Unknown to us Goose Bay was then a militarised zone and was home to the 95th Strategic Wing of the U.S. Air Force. It was connected with the Distant Early Warning (D.E.W. Line) system and was part of a screen of such bases stretching up the North American coast to East Greenland and Iceland, the object being to detect and allow a rapid response to a Soviet attack which, in those days, seemed a distinct possibility. Having landed up in the middle of this highly restricted military area, nobody seemed to notice us. Our only aim was somehow to get up-country to fish, but we could find no way of doing this. We wandered around making enquiries about flights out but to no avail. When we were hungry we simply went along to a military canteen and had a slap-up American-style meal.

At nightfall we wandered over to a runway and, within a stone's throw of some sinister-looking grey British built strategic 'V' bombers, we scraped hollows in the sand and bedded down almost under the wing of a Valiant bomber which, for all we knew, was loaded with atom bombs. At night the dismal howling of coyotes filtered through into our dreams and in the morning we woke not much refreshed. The next day was spent in more fruitless searching for a way out of the base and that night we slept in a derelict bus which we found in a hanger.

On the third day we were getting desperate and for light relief went to see the film 'Journey to the Centre of the Earth' in the military cinema. Bizarrely one of the first figures on the screen was myself, complete with period costume. A few years previously, when a student, I had acted as an 'extra' when part of the film was shot at Edinburgh University. That night it was the bus again.

The following day we were discovered and were taken into custody for questioning. Our story must have sounded highly improbable and the interview was somewhat unfriendly. The upshot was that we were given one hour to get off the base. Thanks to the kindness of Jo Luckley, the nurse in charge, we spent a night in the Grenfell Mission in the nearby village of Happy Valley. The next plane out was a DC4 freighter with eight military personnel as passengers. The trouble was that it was going to yet another military base, but this time 700 miles to the north in Baffin Island in the Canadian Arctic. However, we had no option but to go along but it turned out to be a very relaxed journey during which we wandered amongst the freight and chatted to the pilot. Beneath us the bog and spruce-dotted 'muskeg' and rivers of Labrador remained tantalisingly beyond our reach.

It was dusk when we landed at Frobisher on Baffin Island which looked the bleakest place on earth. The settlement was partly militarised and when our fellow soldier passengers disembarked we simply shouldered our rucksacks and followed them to the barrack huts. Everyone, including ourselves, was designated one out of a long line of beds. On my right was a black American soldier from Idaho and on the left a tough-looking soldier from the Bronx. They were all very pleasant but could not understand how we came to be there and for that matter neither could we. Things seemed to be slipping into the realms of unreality. This was meant to be a fishing trip but it was assuming a Kafka-esque atmosphere with a momentum of its own.

Our break came when, next day, we absconded without leave from the military and went to the local Royal Canadian Mounted Police post. The Mounties were most helpful and sat us down in the office, in which there was a cage, complete with a resident villain peering through the bars. Apparently the Sylvia-Grinnell river was not far away and at that time of year was filled with migratory arctic char. We had caught these beautiful fish in Iceland and Norway and this sounded like a marvellous opportunity. From this point everything went right. The Department of Northern Affairs gave us keys to small unfurnished empty cabin for no payment and the Mounties sold us fishing permits for 2 dollars each. It seemed great luxury to have a roof over our heads even though we had to sleep on the floor.

There was plenty to look at during the two mile walk to he river. On our left the sea was dotted with distant ice floes and, far off, the hills of a grey rock-bound coast hid the view to open water. Ahead of us, across a landscape of tundra and rock, we could see a gleam of white where the river cascaded into the sea at the head of an inlet and at our feet were clusters of arctic flowers. It was a beautiful scene - until we almost stumbled over six dead huskies or sledge dogs which had been shot. Presumably they had become surplus to requirements.

As we came closer we could see that the river formed a series of cascades over rocks before plunging into a long, narrow sea inlet. Just above the level of the sea a rock basin with white water surging through it was filled with a mass of jostling char. Dorsal fins and tails flipped and splashed above the surface continuously and sometimes a fish itself was shouldered half out of the water. In Alaska such a spot would attract bears, but here, instead, stood an Inuit boy pulling out fish with a huge treble hook on a hand line.

During the next few days we caught about a dozen char, some of them quite big, using red and white spoons but I wish that I had tried a fly. They ranged from 5lbs upwards and we had two of 12 lbs. They fought furiously, were absolutely beautiful to look at and were very good to eat. We kept one or two for ourselves and gave others to the Inuit boy who became our self-appointed ghillie and who, when necessary, paddled us across the sea inlet in a minute, leaky homemade boat which was kept afloat only by bailing.

One day an odd thing happened. I was fishing just where the river plunged into the salt water and in the turbulence, out of the corner of my eye, I glimpsed what seemed to be a really big char breaking the surface. My first cast over the place was rewarded with an almighty pull. I could not make any real impression on whatever it was and it gradually took my line further and further towards the open sea while I followed as best I could. I tried standing and exerting maximum pressure but was rewarded only with massive tugs. Nothing I could do seemed to alter progress down the inlet. After about half an hour the line started to grate on some underwater object and then everything stopped. After one or two more great tugs the line parted and that was that. I will never know what I had on, but possibly it was some marine fish or mammal which had been preying on the char, perhaps a seal but it never appeared to surface for air.

Our self appointed Inuit boy ghillie with a pair of arctic char, biggest 12lbs, which we caught in the Sylvia Grinnell River, Baffin Island in 1960.

Up to this time we had been subsisting on an almost entirely fishy diet and we developed a longing for something different. On the way back to our house that day we happened to pass what must have been a cook-house, for through the open window wafted a delicious smell of baking. We peered inside where a cook was taking something out of an oven and we asked if he could spare a dry crust. He took one look at our rather dishevelled figures and said, "You know what you are, you're a couple of professional bums," and with that he passed through the window an enormous freshly-baked blueberry pie!

After a few days the char population in the sea pool diminished as the fish moved on upstream and our thoughts turned to the possibility of finding other rivers. By chance we heard that an Inuit hunter called Inooki was about to go on a seal hunt out into the pack ice and he agreed to take us along. He was to be away for many days and we thought that this might be a good chance to scout the coast for char fishing. His open 18 foot Hudson Bay Company issue canoe was devoid of any comforts, but the sides had been heightened by 6 inches with nailed-on plywood. He was armed with a pump action .22 rifle and a powerful Winchester 270 which would be useful in the event of meeting polar bears which occur around the Baffin coast. Sometime previously, while in the reclining position, he had shot at a seal using his extended leg as a rest - quite forgetting that, although the view through the telescopic sight was well above leg level, the bullet trajectory was not - and he blew his leg off! However, the wooden version seemed to function adequately. He was a moody individual and spoke virtually no English.

We set off on the day that the first icebreaker ship, the 'Sir William Alexander', got through to Frobisher. On the way out we pulled alongside and several crew members shouted down to us that

The canoe in which we lived and travelled through the pack ice off Baffin Island.

we were crazy to go into the ice in such a frail boat. In retrospect they were right and we got no further than two miles out when the ancient Seagull outboard motor had its first of many breakdowns. It was a long paddle back to the ship where an engineer tried, unsuccessfully to do a repair job and we returned to base.

Two days later at 3am. Inooki woke us, the gasket having been 'repaired' with lead from an old pipe and we were off! At first only scattered ice floes lay on the mirror calm sea. In bright sunshine the white tops merged into turquoise as the water reflected sunlight below icy overhangs. The further we travelled the thicker the pack-ice became. One of us was appointed ice lookout in the bows, an important job since ramming a lump of ice could easily sink us. Inevitably we sometimes did crash into partially submerged floes but fortunately the resultant torrent was furious Inuit invective rather than seawater. We threaded our way among extraordinary icy sculptures; an almost perfect white camel was succeeded by a floe topped with an upright icy frame as though waiting for a painting to fill the void. Later a raft of ice with a scarlet stain showed where a polar bear had killed and eaten a seal. We learned to recognise floes which originated from Greenland glaciers as these provided our fresh drinking water.

Soon we began to encounter what were common, or possibly, harp seals. At the first sight of a head Inooki stopped the engine and, in the silence, scratched on the side of the canoe. The seal, being inquisitive, would come closer to investigate, only to be greeted with a Winchester bullet or sometimes a hail of bullets from the .22. When the head exploded in a crimson plume the engine was 'gunned' and the carcase retrieved before it sank. The young seals, especially, had beautiful spotted silver coats and were much prized by the Inuit women. After travelling for about nine hours, dense fog descended and it was impossible to keep a sense of direction among the floes, some suddenly looming twenty feet above our heads. When the dark shadow of an island appeared out of the fog we gratefully pulled the canoe onto a desolate grey beach.

Inooki retrieving a seal shot with his Winchester 270.

Skinning seals. The liver and meat were almost our sole sources of food.

Later when the fog had thinned the journey continued but the engine again broke down: it seemed to be gasket trouble once more and Inooki's attempts at repair did not inspire confidence and I felt the first hint of concern for our safety. After an hour the engine spluttered into life and we continued. Ice conditions were difficult and at one point near some islands the floes around us were swept along by a current and predictably the engine again failed. Drifting along amid huge masses of ice without propulsion was unnerving, but fortunately another temporary repair allowed us to continue and to search for a camp site on an island.

It was dusk by the time we found a small beach and quickly put up the tent securing it with rocks while Inooki arranged his own shelter. In that part of the arctic bleached driftwood abounds having been carried from Siberia in the circumpolar current and using this, a good fire was soon lit. Supper of boiled seal liver helped to make us feel better but we were perpetually cold and before settling into sleeping bags we heated boulders in the fire and buried them in the sand under our groundsheets. Although they tended to melt the

Treacherous fog in the pack ice was a serious problem and it was a relief to find refuge on an island.

Washing out the canoe after a hunt.

groundsheets they gave a little temporary warmth. Unnervingly the silence of the night was intermittently filled with appalling booming roars as some floe broke up or capsized and the awful sound echoed back and forth in the darkness. I never quite got used to that noise; it made us feel so puny beside what nature could do.

We were just settling into a half frozen sleep when something else jolted us into wakefulness. A wolf's howl drifted through the darkness on one side of the camp and then, alarmingly loud and close by on the other side. The sound of wolves is disturbing enough when heard from a distance, but this was close, very close, and there was clearly quite a number of them. At once Inooki, obviously very afraid, shouted urgently to break camp and in the darkness our things were bundled into the canoe in a great hurry. He was quite panicky and paddled us a hundred yards out where we tied up to an ice-floe. I had always understood that wolves do not attack humans, but Inooki

Marooned by ice. A cold camp on the desolate coast of Baffin Island where heated rocks buried under the tent at night provided transient warmth.

indicated that they become marooned on islands when the sea ice breaks up and when they run out of food they are, indeed, dangerous.

What remained of that night was thoroughly cold, uncomfortable and miserable. The three of us lay on the bottom of the canoe in which an inch or two of water, red with seal blood, slopped around. I used a small seal as a pillow, but sleep was out of the question as I developed stomach cramps and now and then had to rush out onto the floe for obvious reasons. To add to our woes icy rain started to fall and Inooki rigged up a tarpaulin shelter held up by a paddle and beneath it set up a primus stove to brew coffee. David remonstrated when he placed the stove on top of a 20 gallon drum of petrol, but ignoring him, our trusty hunter proceeded to pump the primus to get it going, whereupon a fountain of flaming paraffin enveloped not only the primus but also the drum of petrol. It seemed probable that we were about to be blown to smithereens and all three of us beat at the flames with clothing and anything else that came to hand and only after few anxious minutes was the conflagration put out though the drum continued to steam and smoke for a few more moments. The concept of health and safety was not uppermost in Inooki's mind and we spent the rest of that awful night with his loaded rifles pointing at us from his end of the canoe. The thought of being drilled through from feet to the top of the head in no way contributed to our peace of mind.

The ensuing days were chiefly devoted to hunting and simply surviving rather than searching for new rivers to fish. We lived on seal liver and meat and ate some raw char which we had brought with us. We did see one small river but Inooki would not stop to investigate it. On one island we were sent out with a rifle to try to supplement our diet of seal meat, and although we saw some ptarmigan and a white hare, we returned empty-handed. Inooki was a remarkable shot and one day downed a flying goose with the Winchester. Later, less skilfully, he shot up a nest of gulls, and took several home to his wife.

One evening we beached for the night on an island beside two deserted Inuit shacks made of stones, turf, pieces of driftwood, sacking and bits of polythene. Inside, a jumble of animal skins lay on the floor as bedding and although Inooki said that we could sleep there, the smell was so overpowering that we chose our tent. Outside a great heap of bleached seal and other much larger bones was evidence of good hunting in previous years and beside this lay a long dead dog.

The density of the ice floes was always a source of anxiety and five days later when we tried to head back to Frobisher the way was blocked. Gradually we were edged away from the Baffin mainland as the ice closed in and had to take refuge on Bruce Island. Next day progress was slow as we had repeatedly to climb some of the higher floes to search with binoculars for leads through the pack-ice.

Ultimately we made it back to the Inuit settlement at Frobisher. On approaching the shore Inooki gave some shrill blasts on what he called his 'wife whistle' and at once his wife and a clutch of little

Inooki searching for leads of open water through the ice.

children hurried to meet us. They pulled the seals over to some flat rocks and began to cut them up along with the other proceeds of the hunt. Clearly Inooki had performed his role and now it was up to the women and children.

With some relief we returned to our quarters, perhaps a little surprised that we had survived. The hunt had been an interesting experience, appallingly uncomfortable and, I think, dangerous at times, but neither of us would have wished to have missed it.

The time had arrived to search for fishing elsewhere: a plane was due to depart for Fort Chimo by Ungava Bay, and that seemed as good a place as any to try out. After a 400 mile flight we landed in the Inuit settlement surrounded by spruce trees and lakes - so different from the rock and tundra of Baffin. A mile or so into the forest we pitched the tent beside an attractive lake and in a nearby creek David caught nine nice little trout which rapidly found their way into our frying pan.

Back at Frobisher Inooki's work was done and the women and children dealt with the seals.

Our final fishing foray was to the area of Lake St.John in Quebec. We particularly wanted to fish for ouananish or landlocked salmon which are found in various parts of Canada and the Ashuapmushuan River, in particular, was said to hold good numbers of this curious fish. Over the millennia the species has lost its way to the sea and from the lake the fish run up the river to spawn. A 700 mile flight to Roberval on Lake St.John brought us within easy reach of our goal. The Ashuapmuchuan turned out to be very big with a huge surge of peat stained water. It was difficult to know where to fish, so we pitched the tent and tried some of the quieter water along the banks. I could not visualise a fly succeeding and we managed to catch two ouananish of 3lbs each with a spoon. It was not an ideal way to catch these attractive fish, but effective. Their shape was exactly the same as that of an ordinary salmon, but they were brownish rather than silver. The flesh was pink but not as oily as a sea-going

Cut off from land by dangerous moving ice which threatened to crush the canoe.

A 3lb landlocked salmon (ouananish) from the Ashuapmuchuan

salmon, but roasted on a stick over the camp fire as the Saami had taught us in Finnmark they were delicious.

This then was nearly the end of an eventful trip, though a final jaunt took us to Montreal and then across Canada by rail to Jasper in the Rockies..

I am very aware that this account is as much about travel and adventure as about fishing but fishing acted as the central purpose round which everything else took place. On the way to Jasper we happened to share a railway compartment with a charming itinerant Irishman who asked why on earth we had been wandering around northern Canada. When we explained, he was silent for a long while, and then said in his broad Irish brogue -"You're right. You've got to have a purpose."

After this I returned to Edinburgh to continue my medical studies but David went on to New Zealand still clutching his rod.

Chapter 5

African Trout

In 1962 when I graduated from Edinburgh University Medical School life suddenly looked a bit more serious. Long vacations, usually taken up with fishing expeditions, might be a thing of the past but as a last fling a relation, Harry Usher, and I decided to do some travelling in Africa. Harry was to start in Sudan and I was to join him a little later in Uganda and from there we would make our way as best we could to Capetown. The journey, sadly, was curtailed for Harry when he contracted amoebic dysentery and had to be hospitalised in Rhodesia. He was really quite ill but after a month and a series of operations he was just well enough to travel home in one piece.

The possibility of fishing in Africa seemed remote but nevertheless our host in Kenya offered to take us trout fishing on the Sosiane River on the slopes of 14,173 foot high Mount Elgon, on the Kenya-Uganda border. Apparently rainbow trout were introduced to the continent early in the twentieth century and even in tropical Africa they thrived, but only in cool high altitude mountain streams.

We set off early one morning in a Land Rover with borrowed fly rods accompanied by that very African sound of shrilling cicadas in the overhead trees. During the ascent on the rough track the landscape changed strikingly with increasing altitude. On the lower ground we came across a troupe of black and white colobus monkeys sitting peacefully in the canopy of a large tree. Higher up the mountain the forest was tangled with lianas. Beards of moss and lichen hung from almost every branch and wisps of vapour or cloud hung among the trees. Now and then brilliant tree orchids gave blinks of colour in the shade of the forest and there were glimpses of brightly coloured birds and butterflies.

In due course we came across the Sosiane which was little more than a mountain stream rushing through thick forest and across open glades. At 9000 feet the track was blocked with fallen trees brought down by elephants and we had to clear the way with axes, an unusual way to go trout fishing.

We started to fish where the river ran through dense bamboo thickets, criss-crossed by tracks made by elephant and buffalo and it was these tracks which, on foot, we had to use to move along the river. The passageways were only just elephant-width and the horrible possibility of meeting one of the monsters or a buffalo kept us on the alert. Some of the droppings looked alarmingly fresh.

The water of the Sosiane was brown with suspended sediment and I was surprised to see numerous freshwater crabs scuttling along the edge of the stream. We were told that the trout feed on the juvenile crustacea but my fly box contained nothing resembling a small crab. Not knowing what a young crab looked like I began by trying a dull coloured fly which proved to be quite ineffective. On reflection it seemed to me that perhaps something shiny might work in view of the muddy water and I ended up by cutting a little oval of silver metal from the lid of the fly box which I impaled onto the hook of the fly. This invention proved to be highly effective and before long a lively little rainbow trout of half a pound was on the bank. We fished for several hours and caught eight beautiful fish, some of which were about the pound mark.

It had been a delightful day and on our return it was nicely rounded off by ice cold gins and tonics on our host's verandah. Fishing in Africa seemed to have a lot to recommend it, a far cry from the many cold rainy days which I have spent on Scottish waters. Not for a minute did I think that the very next year we would be back in Africa once again doing a little impromptu trout fishing, though this time in Morocco.

The following year Harry and I, along with another friend, John McCulloch, decided that it would be fun to go on a mountain scrambling trip to the High Atlas Mountains of Morocco where we especially wanted to climb the 13,670 foot Jebel Toubkal. I had heard that trout exist in some of the mountain lakes there, so I had packed a fly rod and one or two trout flies - just in case - though I must say that trout and North Africa sounded an unlikely association.

We approached the mountains through Marrakesh in a local bus and later hired some mules which took us up the foothills. What wonderful beasts they were, surefooted and patient, as they carried us along sometimes precipitous, narrow paths. After that we walked. The sun shone relentlessly and overheating was a problem. Once, when resting by a rock, something moving just beside my face turned out to be a warty chameleon observing me with its unnervingly independent eyes.

At nightfall we camped beside a beautifully cool, rushing stream and at this higher altitude the presence of trout did not altogether seem an impossibility after all. The water looked clear and pure and quenched our considerable thirst. However, at dawn the next day a chanting voice woke us and through the open tent flap we could see a local man wearing a djellaba saying his prayers on the bank of the stream after which he urinated into the water just above the camp. On our way through the mountains that day, we sighted another Berber tending a herd of goats, but when we ran to catch up with him he took fright and fled. After a short pursuit he stopped and seemed mightily relieved to find that we only wanted some goat's milk which was provided on the spot from the udders of a willing nanny in exchange for some matches. Mindful of the risk of brucellosis we treated the milk with a liberal handful of water purifying tablets.

The following day while scrambling through a dry, rock-strewn landscape, we came upon a little emerald green lake nestling in a hollow. It hardly looked like trout water, but nevertheless we climbed down to have a look. The green colour seemed to be caused by algae, but it was still possible to see about 18 inches to the stony bottom. To my surprise, here and there on the surface, little dimples suggested that, after all, there might indeed be trout in the lake, or at least fish of some kind.

Having retrieved my rod from our camp, I put on the smallest trout fly that I had, took off my boots, socks and trousers and waded in. Some of the best rises were fairly well out and after casting among them for half an hour, I had several attractive little trout. We were quite glad to have these as our diet in the mountains did not include any protein and the thought of a nice trout fry-up was a marvellous prospect.

As I fished on I noticed a number of dimples in the shallower water between me and the shore and I cast among these but without effect. The little dimples continued all around me and I thought this a bit odd, so after winding in the line, I bent down and peered into the water. Then, not a yard from me, I clearly saw a snake - a viper - appear from the submerged stones and its head reached up to the surface, dimpling it as it took in air, before shrinking back to its lair on the bottom. Then I saw another just beside me, its triangular head and black zig-zag markings leaving no room for doubt that I was, indeed, standing barefoot in a nest of vipers! The thought of being bitten on the foot, or even elsewhere, was unappealing and I developed a strong urge to get out of the water as fast as possible. I made a mad rush for it back to the security of my boots and, unusually for a fisherman, I was glad that some of the inhabitants of the lake were not biting that day.

The mules coping with atrocious terrain in the Atlas Mountains.

RUSSIA

ALASKA

CANADA

BERING
SEA

Anchorage

Lake Iliamna

Kvichak River —————— •King Salmon

NORTH
AMERICA

KING SALMON
ALASKA

Chapter 6

Salmon and Bears in Alaska

All my life I have kept a fishing record book and for the 5th August 1990 there is an entry of lunch at 32,000 feet over the Hebrides on the way to fish in Alaska. Beside me was my old surgical colleague and friend Jimmy Thomson and in front of us some recently emptied glasses of gin and tonic. Our fellow passengers, mostly dark-suited Japanese on their way to Tokyo, observed our high spirits in inscrutable silence. We had good reason for enthusiasm as Alaska is one of the most extraordinary fishing destinations in the world with five species of Pacific salmon and some of the finest rainbow trout in existence. As if that is not enough the rivers and lakes abound with a variety of char known as dolly varden, grayling and various other species. I have always enjoyed the thrill of anticipation of such a journey and judging by the splashes of British Airways' Cote du Ventouse on my record book that lunch was a good one.

It would be short sighted to go to Alaska just for the fishing as the landscape and fauna are unique and contribute greatly to the enjoyment of a trip. The wilderness has really changed little since prehistoric times and abounds with wildlife. Herds of caribou still migrate across the tundra and in summer bears and wolves forage and hunt along the rivers, while moose browse in the marshes. Massive shoals of migrating salmon show up as huge dark stains in the rivers when viewed from 300 feet up in a float plane and provide a vital influx of protein into the interior of Alaska without which the ecosystem would collapse. Bears, wolves and bald eagles gorge on salmon in summer and help to convert the protein into nitrogen

Glaciers near the Alaskan coast.

which, when spread along river valleys, promotes growth of plants and trees.

Our destination, No See Um Lodge, timber built and most comfortable, overlooks the Kvichak River 25 miles from the sea. It really is in the middle of nowhere. The river drains the huge Lake Iliamna which lies 30 miles upstream and is the migratory pathway for hordes of salmon. At the lodge the river is about 300 yards wide and is ideal for the two Cessna float planes moored at the landing stage and, using these, we were able to fish different rivers each day.

We flew up from Anchorage to King Salmon on the coast and were met by our host, Jack Holman, with the float plane. The half hour trip to the lodge gave us a foretaste of the terrain of forest and tundra. After a quick lunch our rods were inspected. My 15 foot fly-rod was rejected out of hand and we were given little lightweight 8 foot 'wands' instead and were asked what we wanted to fish for that afternoon. "Well, salmon of course," was our reply and we were shortly on our way in a Cessna to a spot a few miles downstream. The plane landed beside a gently shelving beach backed by head high

The Cessna on the Kvichak provided daily transport to other rivers.

grass and undergrowth. We were told to try that stretch, but to look out for bears. Clearly there were plenty of bears about and here and there in the sand were enormous clawed footprints. Rather alarmingly I later found one into which water was still seeping though I had neither seen nor heard the beast responsible.

Grizzly footprint.

Jimmy and I fished from that beach for about two hours and caught no fewer than 30 salmon between us, all of which were returned to the water. Two were chum salmon of around 10 lbs and the rest humpbacks all about 5lbs. They took an outlandish pink fly which we christened the Barbara Cartland and fought well enough, but there was really no point in fishing on as it was all just too easy. Seeing that we wanted more of a challenge Jack suggested that we should concentrate instead on Alaska's magnificent rainbows and this proved to be good advice.

The following morning a Cessna was ready for us at the landing stage and beside it stood our ghillie-pilot. The contrast between a traditional Scottish ghillie and Harley could not have been more marked. Instead of tweeds he wore a blue shirt and a scarlet baseball cap and in place of a landing net he carried a black pump-action shotgun as protection against bears. The take-off from the river, as always, was exhilarating and soon we had a wonderful view of the tundra with its scattered groups of spruce trees and lakes. We were going to try the quite small Gertrude River on this, our first day, where rainbow trout and char abound. After thirty minutes flying time the silver coiled river lay beneath us and Harley brought the plane down smoothly on one of

Harley, our ghillie, with his bear gun.

the few straight stretches. The Gertrude was an attractive little river with plenty of rocky runs and glides. Along it grew clumps of shoulder high willow which relieved the barren landscape and in the far distance snow-patched mountains formed the horizon.

The rainbows and char gather just below spawning salmon and feed on the eggs as soon as the hen fish releases them and not surprisingly the best pattern of 'fly' resembles a pink egg. These pink beads are fished nymph-style by casting upstream and allowing the bead to trundle, impeded, close to the bottom. We were using 8lb nylon and very light rods and what enormous fun we were to have. Before long I was into a rainbow which played spectacularly and jumped four or five times. When it was played out at my feet I could see just how beautiful these fish really are. Although only about 5lbs it was broad with a firm, almost hard, body with no suggestion of the soft floppiness of farmed rainbows and along the flanks glowed a pink iridescent sheen. It was carefully unhooked and, like all our rainbows, was returned to the water seemingly little the worse for the experience. During the day I had seven similar fish, but much larger ones are not uncommon - some up to 10lbs. We also caught numerous dolly varden, a variety of char and they too were most attractive looking fish. As well as this we had a number of good sized grayling. The sport was fast and furious and when I once tried to photograph Jimmy playing a fish, a rainbow took my own 'fly' which I had left trailing in the water. This made it impossible to use the camera so I simply gave my rod to Jimmy and I now have an amusing series of pictures of him playing two fish simultaneously with a pair of rods.

An odd thing happened that day. In the morning I hooked and played out a dolly varden of about 4 lbs. and just before removing the hook, I carelessly grasped the nylon which promptly broke and the fish escaped. Later in the afternoon we were working our way back to the plane and had reached to about the same place when a fish took. It played strongly for a time and when it was ready I drew it into the shallows and removed the hook. However, clearly the fish was still

Dolly varden char waiting to be returned.

*Jimmy Thomson trying to cope with two fish on the little Gertrude River.
One was a big rainbow and the other a dolly varden*

attached to the line and had to be played for another few minutes. It turned out that I had removed the morning's hook and the fish, evidently a slow learner, had gone for the bead again in spite of already having had a sharp lesson. I am not convinced that fish suffer much pain when being caught and this little episode confirms in my mind that they probably do not.

The following day we were flown out to the Kulik River which is much larger than the Gertrude and where we used a fly known as a Sculpin which is tied with olive green feathers. Once again the day produced numerous rainbows of up to 6lbs. Parts of the river were packed with huge numbers of sockeye salmon in their spawning colours which glowed red in the water like enormous goldfish. Some had evidently completed spawning and the banks were littered with their disintegrating bodies. The mass death of Pacific salmon is extraordinary to watch and a few days later I was wading down a clear gravely river surrounded by hundreds of spawning red sockeye. Every now and then one of them would suddenly float belly up and drift away downstream. Occasionally one would take our fly though we tried to

Sockeye in their spawning colours looked like goldfish in the pools.

A Sockeye near spawning time; hardly a beautiful sight and we tried to avoid catching them.

Dead sockeye littered the edge of the stream.

avoid this as much as possible as at this stage of their life they are far from attractive. Their dull green under-parts are offset by bright red backs and the up-tilted elongated jaws give an alligator-like appearance.

Most of us have experienced an 'unforgettable' day's fishing and there was one particular episode on this trip that I will not forget in a hurry. That day we were to fish American Creek, a quite small heavily forested river in the company of our host Jack Holman. From the Cessna we could see the river flowing among thick spruce trees and, descending, we lined up to a calm stretch. As bushes and undergrowth flashed by during landing we passed a surprised grizzly bear which rushed from the river into the cover of the forest, a reminder that even on small rivers there were plenty of bears about.

The fishing again was remarkable and we caught many char and quite a few rainbows. We had been warned not to surprise bears in the forest by coming upon them silently as they can be aggressive when alarmed. The best method seemed to be to chatter away some nonsense to oneself or at least to make some sort of noise. However, at one point I had just caught and landed yet another char. The hook proved a little

Thick forest around American Creek increased the chances of bear ambush.

difficult to remove and in my concentration I was silent for a time. Suddenly there was loud splashing just behind me and on glancing round I saw to my horror that an enormous grizzly was charging straight at me, not more than a dozen paces from where I was crouching with my fish. One cannot possibly outrun a bear, but instinctively, with a shout of alarm, I leapt into the river and headed in a plunging rush for the opposite shore. Fortunately my shout alerted Jack 50 yards downstream and, seeing my predicament, he gave a blast on his bear alarm horn. This evidently turned the beast which then vanished into the forest. During my progress across the river yet another rainbow had taken my hook and by the time I arrived on dry land it was charging about the river trailing yards of loose line. Most probably the bear had thought that I was another of his own kind and simply wanted to see me off and to take the fish and the episode would best be described as a bear 'encounter' rather than an attack. Whatever it was my hands were a little shaky for a time!

One morning a quite brisk wind was blowing and prevented use of the Cessnas and for a change we went downstream in a motor boat to try for coho or silver salmon. These beautiful fish run up the rivers a little later in the year than the other species and are especially prized for eating. The trip revealed plenty of interest including white headed bald eagles, ospreys and a golden eagle and most of them were after the same thing as we were - salmon.

On this occasion we were advised to use small spinning rods armed with Pixie spoons. Before long we caught a good many humpback and chum salmon, but then we located the shoals of coho. We caught about half a dozen and they turned out to be very handsome fish of about 10lbs, all of them as silver as a salmon can be and deep bodied so that they looked almost fat. Apart from several of these which we kept for eating we did not kill a single fish on the whole Alaskan trip. In due course we moved to a new spot where the water was very deep and where the first cast resulted in a sharp pull, with a rather macabre result. On retrieving the spoon there was a large eyeball from some unfortunate fish impaled on the point of a hook.

Jimmy Thomson on the Kvichak with coho or silver salmon which run up the rivers later in summer than the other four species.

After an eventful day's fishing we returned to the lodge and on the jetty Harley cleaned the salmon. He beckoned to us to come and watch as he dropped the intestines into the water. As the coiled pale offal sank into the clear water it was suddenly engulfed by an startlingly big shadow which darted up from the depths. More large shadows appeared to join the feast and it seems that they were rainbows which had grown to huge size thanks to regular meals of salmon innards. Unfortunately no fishing was allowed at that place!

One day we flew out to Moraine River which flows through a wide expanse of upland country with distant rounded hills which reminded me of the landscape in Shetland. Save for stunted willow little grew but tussocky grass. The river did not have a suitable place for the Cessna to land but there was a small lake not far away. When we were about to touch down it became clear that the lake really was small and we ended up just short of the rocks of the far shore.

Moraine was one of the best rainbow rivers and again we caught numerous fish, some up to 7lbs, as well as char and grayling. At one point I was fishing from a small beach when a movement opposite caught my eye. There 20 yards from me shambled a large bear. The characteristic humped shoulder of a grizzly sloped down to low hindquarters, giving an almost prehistoric appearance, a sight that must have been familiar to our ancestors in Neolithic times. I quietly backed off and sat on a rock 50 yards away until he disappeared upstream. Later that day several groups of bears arrived where we ourselves were fishing. Fortunately they ignored us but we took care to retreat a good distance until they moved on. They seemed to be after sockeye and chum and some cubs were still learning how to catch fish and though they made a lot of splashing they did not seem to be very successful. When the adults caught a salmon they stripped off and ate the skin which they seemed to prefer rather than the flesh.

Naturally, we were quite wary of bears, as each year bear encounters and attacks are reported in Alaska with a fatality approximately every other year. The largest recorded grizzly, a Goliath of a bear was shot when it allegedly attacked a forestry worker a few years ago. It was said to have weighed over 1,600 lbs. and stood 12 feet 6 inches high at the shoulder. Meeting that nightmare of a bear would certainly have ruined my day's fishing.

It was late afternoon when we walked back to the plane and on approaching a ridge a caribou trotted up to the high ground and stood for a moment, silhouetted against the sky, its wide antlered head striking a pose worthy of a Landseer portrait. Then with a bound it vanished

Grizzly. Meeting bears in the open is manageable but problems can arise in thick forest.

Learning to fish.

over the hill. On the way back to the lodge we flew low over a bull moose browsing in a marshy lake, its huge antlers draped with trailing strands of water weed, and later a wolf, eating dead or dying salmon in the shallows of a lake, ran off at the approach of the plane.

That day was our last and, in the comfort of the lodge where we had been so wonderfully looked after by Jack and his wife, we had time to reflect on all that had happened. When we had initially arrived in Anchorage we had seen notices advertising 'The Alaskan Experience' and the term rather nicely sums up the essence of our time there. Ours did not turn out to be just a fishing trip after all; there was much more to it than that. Although I will never forget the magnificent rainbows, salmon and char which we caught, neither will I forget the still beauty of the woods along the rivers, sometimes aflame with a carpet of fireweed, or the seemingly endless open wilderness hemmed by distant snow-streaked mountains - all with the added frisson of knowing that, like our ancient ancestors, we were not top predators in that world of wild animals and we just had to watch our backs.

Sometimes the riversides glowed with fireweed.

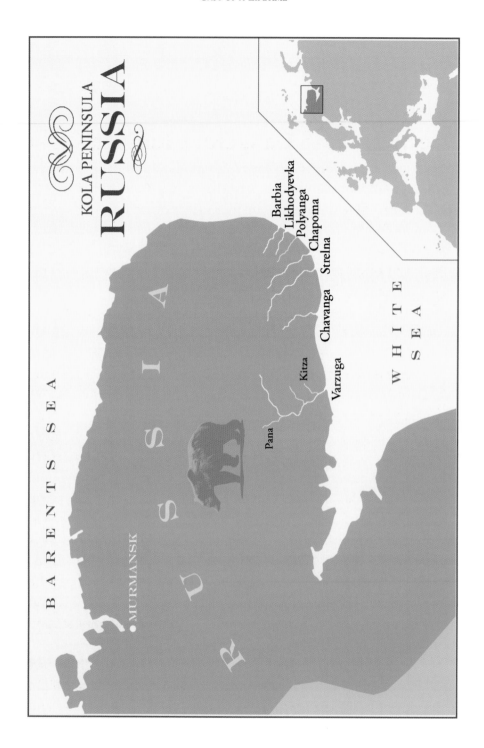

Chapter 7

The Strelna - A Dangerous Russian River

September 15th. 1959

Dear Mr.Kruschev,

I am a third year medical student at Edinburgh University and am very keen on salmon fishing. I believe that there must be some great salmon rivers in northern Russia and I am writing to ask whether it might be possible to obtain permission to fish some of these........

This is part of a letter which I sent to the Kremlin after having fished some of the rivers of Finnmark in North Norway in 1959. According to the map there were scores of likely rivers on Russia's adjacent Kola Peninsula and though I hardly expected a favourable reply it seemed worth taking a chance. My expectations were amply fulfilled - I did not get a reply! This was hardly surprising as the Cold War was at its height and Nova Zemlya in the arctic was being developed by the Soviet Union as its main nuclear test site. As well as this the Kola Peninsula was a militarised zone and in those days nuclear war with the Soviet Union seemed a distinct possibility. However, little did I think that thirty-four years later I would pay the first of twelve visits to fish the magnificent rivers of the Kola and would be privileged to enjoy some of the world's best Atlantic salmon fishing.

Travelling to and within Russia on a fishing trip usually turned out to be an adventure in itself. In the earlier years a Finnair flight took us from Helsinki to Murmansk and was always impeccable and efficient in the Scandinavian manner, but as soon as the plane touched down on the Murmansk runway it was obvious that we really were in Russia. Sometimes there were several touchdowns as the plane banged and leapt along the corrugated runway, but it would be unkind to blame the Russians for this as the permafrost can cause ground-heave. Dotted around the edge of the runway there were usually several antique biplanes in which Biggles would have been quite at home, one of which had three engines. Once, when I was fishing, this three-engined dinosaur, a flying anachronism, chugged across the sky so slowly that it seemed inconceivable that it could remain airborne.

At the foot of the gangway we would be 'greeted' unsmilingly by uniformed women officials who firmly directed us into a small cramped holding area within the decaying concrete terminal building. Passport control at Murmansk has always been a source of wonder to me. After queuing for some time one has to stand before a kiosk occupied by a stern lady customs official. Her inspection of the passport and of oneself takes up to ten minutes, though what on earth she does or finds of interest I never discovered in spite of much leaning forward to have a look. Some of my companions find this 'Russian-ness' irksome, but the whole experience can be interesting and entertaining.

The last stage of the journey is by a Russian Mi8 helicopter across the Kola Peninsula which, on the map, is shaped a bit like the eastward-facing head of an octopus with the Barents Sea to the north and the White Sea to the south. We have always fished the White Sea rivers as they have the most prolific runs of salmon, though the fish are not particularly large. If one wanted to catch really big fish the northern rivers would be best. This final stage of the journey to the furthest of the southward flowing rivers involves a 220 mile trip lasting about one and a half hours. The helicopter is inevitably shatteringly noisy and primitive as far as comforts go. Some of the seat belts occasionally work but most lie tangled down the sides of the seats in

Mi8 Russian helicopter on the tundra by the Barbia river in 1993 still bearing its Aeroflot markings.

a mass of rigid webbing and metal buckles which do not seem to match and, in any case, sometimes one has to sit on baggage. However, if one has remembered to bring good ear defenders the trip can be enjoyable.

The view of the tundra from the air can give an indication of how good the fishing is likely to be. A group of four or five friends and I usually go in the first week of June but even then the weather can be bitterly cold, with a mosaic of ice frosted lakes and snowdrifts on the grey rock-strewn landscape below. In these conditions fish tend to be held up in the lower reaches of rivers since much of the potential flow is still locked up as ice on the tundra lakes. Sometimes reindeer, alarmed at the sound of the engines, can be seen bolting for cover of which there is none except distance. Half way through the journey the slope of the land inclines to the south towards the White Sea and silver veins of rivers lined with birch and spruce appear and then the forest begins. Finally the helicopter circles above the fishing camp - a welcome sight after so much travelling with its promise of a large vodka and a meal.

The prime time for the White Sea rivers is the first fortnight in June when fresh fish run in astonishingly large numbers and when the mosquitos have not yet emerged. Our first visit was in July and clouds of enormous mosquitos were everywhere. I fished then wearing surgical rubber gloves and a head net was essential. A lunch time can of beer had to be drunk through the net and every area of skin had to be covered in spite of using mosquito repellent. The disadvantage of beer was that, after half an hour or so, it became necessary to expose a certain small area of skin for a few moments and this was immediately pounced on by an attack group of the pests which was irritating to say the least. Never again did we fish at that time of year.

A group of friends and I fished the Strelna for a week in early June of 1999 and again in 2000. The first occasion was the more successful as spring on the Kola had been exceptionally cold and the tundra lakes were still frozen. This resulted in a relatively modest height of water which held the fish in the lower reaches near the camp instead of enabling them to disappear upstream past the falls. The second visit coincided with milder conditions and melt-water produced a massive flow but fewer fish, as many had run up to higher reaches.

The Strelna is by no means one of the best rivers on the Kola and mostly we fished the very lowest reach adjacent to the White Sea. The river seems almost to have a dual personality. For most of its length it glides peaceably across the tundra and through silent arctic forests, its surface sometimes calm enough to reflect the green spires of the spruce trees. Then, a mile or two from the White Sea, it breaches a rocky ridge where a waterfall thunders down to a harsher open terrain where it becomes a turbulent and sometimes dangerous river. When the water level is high, the flow charges down a succession of deep rock pools, their underwater ledges and cliffs making wading a dance with death. In a final surge of power a torrent of racing water pours for the last half mile through what amounts to a huge sea pool until the flow is gradually stifled by the inertia of the White Sea itself. Even then the river's influence is not spent and for a hundred yards out drowned shingle ridges mark the confines of the flow and it is possible to wade down these and to catch salmon out at sea!

The Strelna camp consists of three or four cabins on a bluff beside the lower part of the river. On our first visit the river shore was lined with huge blocks of ice and the leaden grey White Sea lay just beyond a broken line of stranded ice floes at the river mouth. Half a mile away on a desolate spit of land a group of bleached and mostly empty wooden houses cluster round an ancient wooden church which was wrecked in the madness that followed the Bolshevik Revolution so that now it looks a truly god forsaken place. Our hutted camp was comfortable enough though certainly not luxurious. The guides were all Russian and by this time I had learned to speak some of the language and could converse, if haltingly. At the outset genial relations were established when a guide asked how old I was, and I replied that I was sixteen, momentarily confusing the Russian words for sixteen and sixty. This and other linguistic gaffes caused in a good deal of amusement.

On our first day the temperature was below freezing and before reaching the sea pool snow drifts and ice blocks on the shore had to be negotiated. The river beside the camp is about 100 yards wide with a very heavy current down the middle of the sea pool. The wading was atrociously difficult among masses of underwater boulders. Securely strapped into a life jacket, I selected my biggest double hooked Ally Shrimp with a sinking line to help cope with the heavy water and prayed that that I was not about to end up in the White Sea. The conditions were quite difficult. The wading was terrifying, the rod rings froze up and my hands were numb inside my gloves. However, it is amazing what the sight of moving fish can do

The Strelna. The sea pool's heavy and dangerous flow pours into the White Sea seen in the distance.

to one's spirits. Within ten minutes several fish had shown not far from me and shortly afterwards something plucked at the fly. On casting again the same thing happened and this time I gave a loop of line and my first Strelna fish was 'on'. It ran hard for the fast water where it jumped several times and was clearly beautifully fresh. At that time the Russian guides were not always expert in netting fish and unless restrained tended to swipe at a still active salmon, often with disastrous results. My guide that day was Sasha, a splendid young Russian, who hovered behind me with a net. In my anxiety to forestall a swipe, as the fish was only just starting to tire, I shouted 'No! No!' in Russian which is, of course, pronounced 'Net Net!' Understandably interpreting this as an instruction to use the net he gave an almighty swipe, missed and the fish promptly shot off across the White Sea towards Archangel never to be seen again. Later on we successfully landed three fish of 5, 6 and 9lbs. all of which were returned to the river, relatively undamaged by the barbless hooks.

One day I was again fishing the Sea Pool when a strange thing happened. The weather had warmed up a little and I was enjoying the wonderful feeling of isolation of the northern Russian landscape when the faint sound of a heavy engine drifted across from the birch forest on the opposite shore. The sound grew louder which was odd as there were no roads in the region. Then an ominous clanking accompanied the engine noise and suddenly, what appeared to be a tank, burst out of the trees and, in a mass of foam, charged through the pool just above where I stood and disappeared into the woods on my side of the river. Over the years I have been disturbed in a pool by dogs, otters and swimming children and once by an angry bear, but never before by a tank! It turned out that the vehicle was, in fact, an ex-Soviet Army tracked armoured troop carrier which was sometimes used by Russians living in a settlement along the coast to visit other villages.

That evening Sasha suggested that, for a change, we should try fishing a small river some miles along the coast and to get there we would borrow this troop carrier which had been left parked among the birches near our camp while its crew enjoyed a little vodka with the camp guides. This sounded fun and I volunteered to drive. After stowing the rods on the top, I lowered myself into what seemed like a steel tomb in which there were no concessions to comfort. The engine noise was appallingly loud but, using the driver's two control levers, steering was easy enough. We roared down to the White Sea shore in a cloud of diesel smoke and, with the engine bellowing, proceeded flat out along the grey coast. What a way to go fishing! However our feeling of invincibility was rather spoilt by having to stop twice to hammer track pins back into place. The small river was certainly worth a visit, though while I caught nothing, my companion had a 5lb. fish.

After a few days on our first visit to the Strelna the weather warmed up and fishing became a real pleasure. Encouraged by the conditions a companion, Frank Usher, and I waded out to where the flow of the Sea Pool merged with the salt water and we immediately began to catch fish. To say that they were fresh from the sea would not strictly be true as they had never left it. By shuffling slowly out we could keep to the underwater gravel ridges which marked the edge of the current until we were quite a long way out and all along these bars we took fish, ending up with seven between us. None was very large, the best possibly eight or nine pounds. Interestingly none had sea lice which may be a reflection of the relatively low salinity of the White Sea. We also had some kelts which we never caught in the river proper. In our enthusiasm we ended up quite a long way from land and suddenly realised that the tide, such as it was, was rising. With water uncomfortably close to the tops of our chest waders we teetered on tiptoes back the way we had come with the gravel falling away under our feet and were very glad at last to step onto good Russian dry land.

That day we kept one fish for the camp kitchen and when cleaning it I sliced open the gut and found that a tapeworm was present. This parasite, of the genus Diphyllobothrium, can, as medical students are taught, cause a rare of a type of anaemia in humans. It occurs in many wild salmon and other fish, but cooking or freezing prevents transmission, though eaters of gravdlax made from wild salmon which have not been frozen - beware! It is said that the worm can grow to twenty feet in length in the human gut - what a price to pay for a tasty morsel on a piece of brown bread!

After dinner that evening a member of our party and I decided to visit the village which we had seen on a point not far from the river mouth. This involved a tricky scramble across an inlet filled with huge lumps of ice at the cost of some rather fine knee bruises. The 'village' turned out to consist of about eight ancient wooden houses clustered around the wrecked church. There were no streets and the only living things seemed to be two furry Russian dogs. It would be difficult to imagine a more dismal scene than the village on the edge of that grey coast. After a few minutes two young men in fur hats, one with a gold tooth, emerged from one of the ramshackle houses and, greeting us warmly, insisted that we should come in for a glass of tea. There were two beds in what was obviously the kitchen-cum-living room and a pile of old nets in the corner along with an ancient radio powered by a huge battery. We were made most welcome and were offered but declined to share their supper of tiny flat-fish which were in a frying pan on the stove. They were obviously desperately poor and I doubt that they had much else to eat. They evidently subsisted by fishing and received only very few roubles pay every month as members of the local collective or 'kolkhoz'. They spoke no English and when we left they insisted on presenting me with a 1897 Czarist silver coin and a book in Russian entitled 'Robinson Island' by the Polish author, Arkadi Fidler.

One day it was suggested that we might like to take the helicopter to fish the Strelna twenty miles upstream in the forested part of the river. After a time the pilot descended almost to treetop level above the beautifully streamy river, but no beach could be found sufficiently clear of trees and bushes to allow landing. The very practical Russian solution was for my guide, Sasha, to be let down on a ladder from the hovering helicopter with an axe. In about fifteen minutes he had felled a mass of small willows and we were able to land without incident.

The river offered miles of perfect fly water which four of us fished carefully but without result. No fish were even seen and it seemed likely that the run had not yet reached the stretch but the beautiful scenery made up for it. I put down my rod and wandered deep into the forest - a still world of majestic spruce trees soaring up from a carpet of soft grey lichen. There was not a sound and I sat on a stump to savour the quiet. It seemed as if the trees were watching - and waiting. It was an odd feeling. The spell was broken when of dozens of waxwings appeared in the branches above me, their soft pinkish buff plumage offsetting the brilliant sealing-wax colours on their wings. They were strangely tame and were not in the least alarmed when I got up to go back to the river.

When I was having the last few casts of the day I was startled to hear the bark of a dog. Then out of the trees emerged a wizened old man in a fur hat and with an enormous knife with a carved wooden handle in his belt. His worn clothes had come to look like blackened leather and a dog sniffed along beside him. He had heard the helicopter and had come to investigate. Apparently he had lived all his life in the forest , sustaining himself by trapping and fishing and eating berries - a so called 'ochotnik' or hunter. We gave him some of our salmon flies but he was mostly fascinated with the helicopter. When it was time for us to take off no-one, unfortunately, had thought to warn him to stand well back and as he waved good-bye the down-draught from the rotors blew him over backwards. I was sorry about that as he was a dignified old man.

Fishing the Chapoma.

A beautifully shaped 12 lb fish from the Chavanga.

Frank Usher with a fish on the Chavanga in 1999. Snow drifts still persisted into early June that year.

We were fortunate in having the helicopter at our disposal at the Strelna, allowing us to fish other rivers including the Polyanga, Chavanga and Chapoma. These are all lovely rivers in magnificent spruce, birch and aspen forest and we caught fish in all of them. On the banks of the Chapoma a companion and I were pushing our way through a birch wood and came upon fresh bear scratchings on a tree-trunk and later found a bear paw print in a patch of snow.

I much enjoyed our trips to the Strelna even though it is a difficult river to fish and sometimes dangerous in high water conditions. We did not catch a large number of fish and the most taken by one rod in a week was twenty, almost all of which were returned. Numerically this is a modest result but we took time to enjoy the natural environment and the people and also the feeling of the strangeness of that extraordinary country which, for me, carries ever present undertones of its terrible history.

Chapter 8

The Varzuga - The River with a Smile

It is difficult to think of a more pleasant river to fish than the Varzuga. Like the Strelna it too runs from Russia's Kola Peninsula into the White Sea and throughout its length it is mostly shallow and gravelly - an ideal spawning ground for salmon. The lightly peat stained water is filtered by a large population of freshwater mussels whose empty, blue shells are often found lying in the gravel by the shore. A huge number of salmon enter the system during the short spring and summer seasons, some of which run up the two main tributaries, the Kitsa and Pana, which are outstanding salmon rivers in their own rights.

For many years the fishing agents, Roxton Bailey Robinson, now known as Roxtons, ran three fishing camps on the Varzuga itself and for six years a group of friends and I have fished from the upper camp where the river is a perfect size. For sheer numbers of fish caught these higher reaches do not compare with the two camps further downstream, but Upper Varzuga is such fun to fish with its glorious gliding pools near the camp and upstream there is a succession of rocky pools, rapids and small cascades. The scenery around this rough-water stretch is especially beautiful. On each bank the shearing action of ice in spring has shaved the vegetation to a few inches in height sometimes for up to ten paces from the water's edge then, out of range of the ice, young spruce trees grow among rocks as if part of a well planned ornamental garden.

When the ice breaks up in mid May the frozen river becomes a grinding mass of moving floes and then spring and summer move fast as if aware that, before long, winter will again be snapping at their heels. In early June the birches become suffused with a haze of green leaf buds and a wave of migrating birds fills the woods, some from as far as Africa and the gentle call of cuckoos announces that summer has arrived on the Kola. This and the sweet descending cadence of willow warblers in the riverside forest has come to epitomise, for me, fishing on this river. Some rivers in my mind seem to wear a smile and the Varzuga is one of these.

The salmon, too, have to get a move on as in late September the river freezes again. They even seem to be in a hurry to take a fly, often doing so in spectacular fashion and I sometimes find myself comparing them to the often dour Scottish salmon. Can it be that a century and a half of relentless fishing of Scottish rivers has removed a 'taking strain' of fish from the spawning population and we are left with those which have survived precisely because they tend not to take?

In the earlier years there was a tented camp beside the river in an idyllic spot, but it was abandoned following flooding when a dam of ice floes blocked the river. Subsequently a camp of about a dozen wooden cabins was established on high ground on the opposite bank, complete with a sauna, a dining cabin and a number of cabins for the rods as well as accommodation for the Russian staff.

There are many stretches of the Varzuga which I love to fish but there is one which, for me, is special. To get there, if there is enough water, one of the camp's boats provides transport for two miles upstream to an enormously wide lagoon from which projects a huge hippo-like rock which has been polished over the centuries by ice. Four hundred yards further on at the head of the lagoon some of the most perfect rapids spill into the quiet water. Rapids come in various degrees of turbulence, some violent and dangerous, but these are far from alarming and the pleasantly brisk flow is checked by numerous submerged boulders which give riffles of white water. Salmon lie throughout a full seventy yards of this stretch and down into the lagoon until they are beyond casting reach. It is a pretty spot and the pebbly beach is backed by light open birch and spruce woods.

One day in June 2002 I decided to try my luck there, the only problem being that the water level, while ample for running fish, was little too low for the boat. This meant a fairly long walk in waders but I set off with one of the camp dogs for company which sniffed happily along by my side and swam when I had to wade. We were both enjoying the surroundings when a movement on the opposite shore caught my attention. We stood absolutely still. A large dark shape raised its head to stare across at us. A bear! With a surprisingly agile movement for a big animal it swivelled round and with a shambling run disappeared into the forest. An hour later one of my companions arrived to fish just where the bear had been. I called across to him that he had company in the forest behind him but to this day I am not sure that he believes me!

A perfect Varzuga grilse.

Alexei, our Russian guide on the Varzuga. The taped rod broke in two at the lower ferrule the next day during casting.

After a good hour's walking we reached the rapids and I began to fish at the top of the fast water. My plan was to start with a short line to cover fish lying close to the beach and then to repeat this but with a longer line. The day was pleasantly warm and a good choice of fly seemed to be a No.8 Willy Gunn without a barb, as dictated by the rules on the Kola. It was clearly going to be an eventful day and within a few minutes the first fish took and hurtled downstream into the lagoon where it rushed about for some minutes. One or two other fish, disturbed by its antics, started jumping about but soon it was possible to walk it back towards the beach. There its sides flashed like burnished copper in the peat-stained water but once on the beach its silver perfection became apparent. This one weighed about 7lbs, was a lovely fish and was carefully returned. That day the rapids produced six fish and many pulls and touches. The most effective casts were those made directly across the current inducing the fish to chase the fly as it whipped round. Casting forty-five degrees downstream was not nearly so productive. Giving a loop of line on feeling a touch seemed to be the best way of hooking fish in the fast water, probably as it results in a belly of line downstream which settles the hook into the corner of the mouth.

Later in the day I walked further upstream where there was a beautiful stretch of rocky pools between fast runs and decided to use a little 9 foot rod which I had brought with me. It was not long before a fish took and taking advantage of the very fast, heavy flow it raced downstream. There was no chance of following and the little reel screamed in protest at the speed until, with a jangle of sprockets and springs, its insides flew apart - and of course no fish! This was almost more entertaining than actually catching a salmon but it was late by then and the dog and I decided that it was time to return to the camp. It had been a most enjoyable day in the company of a delightful dog, with six salmon landed amidst lovely scenery, a disintegrating reel - and a bear. What more could one ask for?

There are, of course, many other good fishing spots, some quite near the camp such as Birch Island, Camp Island and Kichisara Junction, but none quite capture the magic of that upper stretch which I fished with the dog for company.

Some fishers who have never been to Russia have the impression that it is simply too easy to catch salmon there and this is reinforced by catch statistics such as those from Middle Varzuga camp where nine rods fishing for six days in early June 2004 caught no less than 1048 salmon - an average of 19 per rod per day! However, this is by no means usual and certainly nothing approaching this is ever achieved on the attractive upstream water that we have fished.

In 2003 and 2008 there were exceptionally cold, late springs on the Kola Peninsula and the ice broke up on the rivers three weeks later than usual. In the first week of June 2003 we met with light snowfalls and sometimes night frosts with the temperature falling as low as -6 degrees Celsius. Until our last day the main run of salmon had not reached the Upper Varzuga and each rod caught only one or two fish per day in spite of fishing hard. On our last day of that cold year, in an effort to locate the head of the run, our guide took my fishing partner, Derek McIntosh, and me about ten miles downstream by boat to a beautiful reach where the current pulls away from a placid pool in a deep, quickening glide before breaking away into rough water below. Within a few casts onto the glide a fish slashed at my fly. He came again to the next cast and he was on, a nice fresh fish of about eight pounds. We had located the run alright and in a few hours I was lucky enough to catch nine lovely fresh fish from the glide itself and Derek too had a number of similar beauties. The fish seemed determined to take the fly, some coming at it time and again before being hooked and all were subsequently released. One or two had healing injuries which, the guide said, were caused by ice floes - so called 'ice fish.'

A so called 'ice fish' crushed by moving river ice floes.

That day, while memorable enough from the fishing point of view, was made so much more enjoyable as a rise in temperature stirred wildlife into activity. While going downstream in the boat we passed groups of wading birds, appropriately named ruffs, at the water's edge, the males fluffing out their collars of neck feathers as they took part in their mating 'leck'. Whooper swans flew off at our approach but on a quiet stretch little phalaropes did not seem to mind our boat and bobbed about the pools quite happily as we passed. A pair of enormous sea eagles soared over the forest while I was fishing, their characteristically heavy beaked heads searching the landscape and once a capercaillie flew over the river. Unexpectedly, in the warming sunshine, I even came across a basking lizard among the stones near the water's edge which seemed an odd animal to find at the Arctic Circle and nearby clumps of frog spawn jellied some ponds near the river. For the first time that week cuckoos began to call, their soft notes complementing the quiet piping of willow warblers. Summer had come.

On pleasant, sunny days it is all too easy to forget that these northern rivers are potentially dangerous and the water is often very cold. On one occasion we nearly had a disaster when an elderly member of the party was fishing the rapids leading into the big lagoon several miles above Upper Varzuga camp. He was an inexperienced fisher and was yet to catch his first salmon. On wading too far into the rapids he found that he was unable to move back upstream away from the depths of the lagoon. The gravel under his feet began to wash away and suddenly he was down in the very cold water without a life jacket. The surging flow carried him on into deep water towards the lagoon where, relinquishing his rod, he managed to embrace a big, partially submerged rock while his guide made frantic efforts to start the boat's engine. Six or seven minutes elapsed before the engine finally came to life and a rescue was effected though his rod was never found. By that time he was suffering from hypothermia and could do little to help himself. Back at the camp he revived in a warm shower but for several hours appeared shocked by his experience. However, a vodka and a good meal restored him to fighting form.

Sometimes less serious emergencies occurred. One day I was trying to hook a fish that had come repeatedly to my fly when one of the camp boats appeared and irritatingly drove straight over the rising fish and pulled in to the shore beside me. In the boat was a fisher from our camp with a particularly large salmon fly securely embedded just above his eye. An impressive amount of blood had run down his face and it was decided that, as a surgeon, I should be the one to deal with the situation. Fortunately at the camp I had a medical pack, complete with surgical gloves, local anaesthetic with instruments including a scalpel - quite over the top for such a trivial procedure. The victim was duly laid out on the dining table and the skin was cleaned with good Stolichnaya Vodka while the camp staff crowded round to watch the 'operation' which was, of course, simple and painless. I am not sure how ethical it was to have an audience but some amusing photographs resulted!

A captain of British industry with an Ally Shrimp above the eye.

One of the pleasures of fishing in Russia is the contact with the guides and camp staff whose attitudes and points of view are so different from those one is used to at home. A good working relationship has been developed between the firm Roxtons and the Russians and this has been brought about with the indispensable help of a local and very influential man, Svetoslav Mikhailovich Kalyuzhen, known familiarly as Svet. Just about everything that happens on that part of the Kola is done with his blessing. In Soviet times he was chairman of the Soviet Collective and, although the political situation has changed, his power and influence have grown so that he seems now to control almost everything except the weather. He is a huge man with a drooping moustache and, curiously, lives in very modest circumstances. Every Russian that I met when fishing deferred to him and as far as I can discover he has brought great benefits to the region. Such a man in Russia needs a bodyguard but he has a small army at his disposal. One evening in camp the word came that Svet was on his way by helicopter and that our dinner might be late as his henchmen might well eat it. In due course the helicopter landed and four or five tough looking paramilitaries in camouflage fatigues wielding Kalashnikovs emerged and fanned out among the tents, followed by the great man himself. It must be said that the men behaved decently and were reasonably friendly and did not eat our dinner! It seemed appropriate to treat Svet with some respect but during a chat he proved to be most affable.

Over the years that we have fished in Russia the guides and camp staff have always been very pleasant and among them there have been some real characters. One guide had fought in Afghanistan while in the Soviet army and another was one of the first emergency workers at the scene of the Chernobyl explosion in 1968 where he received a sub-lethal dose of radiation. One of my favourites was Vladimir Borisovich who spoke not a word of English and was an intrepid bear hunter. The glossy coat of one of his victims hung on the dining cabin wall attesting to his hunting prowess, though I was rather sorry about it as I like bears. At the original tented Varzuga camp the cook was a powerfully built elderly Ukrainian named Ivan. In the Second World War, as a young teenager in the Red Army, he had fought at Koenigsberg, later renamed Kaliningrad, where he was part of a 'snatch squad' which infiltrated behind German lines to bring back enemy soldiers for interrogation. One can imagine their subsequent fate. Ivan had a magnificent singing voice and one night beside the river under the midnight sun he sang in his rich baritone the famous melancholy Russian song 'Stenka Razin', the tune of which was borrowed for 'The Carnival is Over' by The Seekers. It tells the tale of a seventeenth century hero who, having led an uprising, was subsequently captured and executed. It was curiously moving to hear this familiar melody emerging from its true roots in full Slavic magnificence - like a thread from the distant soul of Old Russia. It sent a shiver down my spine.

Ivan, the Russian cook, who had fought at Koenigsberg, now Kaliningrad, in the Second World War and who had a magnificent singing voice.

Chapter 9

Other Russian Rivers

Nowadays travelling with Roxtons to fish on the Kola Peninsula is a smooth, seamless operation, except when going through Murmansk airport itself where things happen at Russian speed. A specially chartered Airbus from London to Murmansk is followed by a helicopter flight to the camp where there is always a drink, or perhaps several, and a good meal waiting.

Things were not always like this and in July 1993 we made our first visit to Russia with a different travel company to fish the Polyanga and other rivers. That year, having flown from London, we spent a night in a Moscow hotel adjacent to the Lubyanka, the infamous KGB headquarters, which squats above the appalling secrets of its execution cellars where thousands of people were tortured and murdered. Next morning we flew north to Kirovsk on the Kola, a town named after Sergei Kirov, a potential rival to Stalin, who was shot in 1934 during the 'Great Terror.' Not, perhaps, a very cheerful start to a fishing trip, but this was Russia.

Among our fellow passengers were a Soviet Army officer resplendent in uniform and gold braid, geologists, mineral prospectors as well as a motley collection of other Russians. During the flight we were served sweet red Caucasian 'champagne' with sturgeon steaks and on a small table by our seat wilting wild flowers in an old lemonade bottle drooped and shed yellow petals during the journey. Across the aisle was a roomy bunk space perhaps intended for senior Soviet officials or 'apparatchiks' overcome by vodka.

From Kirovsk a helicopter flew us over a wilderness of tundra and forest to our tented camp beside the Polyanga river which flows into the White Sea and which is about the size of the middle Spey. It is an attractive river with many pools separated by streamy runs flowing through rocky tundra with occasional clumps of dwarf willow from which we once put up a covey of willow grouse. The camp was unsophisticated but the circular Russian Army tents were businesslike, each with a central wood-burning stove which produced oven-like heat. There was also a mess tent and a screened communal lavatory of dreaded memory. The shower was fed from an overhead water drum heated by a stove which did its job all too well and one of our party was badly scalded and blistered sustaining first degree burns to his back. The food was of the bully beef and tinned peas variety. The whole experience was great fun except for the mosquitos which, in July, were there in their millions and we learned thereafter to fish only in the first fortnight of June before the mosquitos emerge.

That year the helicopter remained in the camp and each day we flew out to different parts of the Polyanga or to one of two other rivers - the Barbia and Likhodyevka. The little Barbia, which in places was only a dozen or so yards wide, was hotching with salmon and was a joy to fish using a single handed rod. A good combination of flies seemed to be an Ally Shrimp on the tail and a floating Bomber on a long dropper which the fish sometimes chased on the surface in a flurry of spray. One day I had eleven fish of 3 to 8lbs all of which were returned.

For some reason in 1993 there was a run of small grilse in the Polyanga and I had fun with them in the outflow of a wide, lagoon-like pool. At the lower end the stream was compressed into an accelerating glassy-smooth glide which curved over a rocky lip before breaking into a waterfall which crashed onto the rocks below. The little grilse, some of only 2lbs in weight, were lying in the curved lip of water, almost at the point where it became free-falling. They came to my fly repeatedly from their cliff-hanging lie and I ended up with four or five beautiful little fish. The slope of the water where they lay

Eleven fish to one rod in a day on the little Barbia - all released.

approached forty-five degrees and it must have been hard work for them to stay put.

There were bigger fish as well in the Polyanga and one of the party, Frank Usher, caught a 16lb salmon and a 6lb sea trout in one day. These were the biggest fish of the two species which were caught that week and went some way to making up for his scalded back. During our six days on the Polyanga, Barbia and Likhodyevka we averaged up to thirty fish per rod - not remarkable by Russian standards but more than enough to keep us busy.

The daily helicopter trip to the different rivers was always interesting and having been dropped at some distant stretch it was pleasant to be left in blissful silence and to be able to enjoy the isolation. At the end of one day's fishing we gathered, as usual, into a group to await the pick-up. Presently we heard the rumble of engines in the distance as the helicopter flew back and forth searching in the wrong place for some considerable time and we were glad when at last we were found. Sometimes one of the camp dogs would come along for the ride and once one of them jumped out onto the tundra as we were boarding for the evening journey back to camp. When we were ready to take off there was no sign of the it but the helicopter departed anyway leaving it to its own devices. I was quite concerned for the poor beast but the following day it reappeared in camp apparently none the worse for a long walk

We came greatly to respect the Mi8 Russian helicopters and the skill of the pilots, and I can recall only one moment of anxiety. When we left the Polyanga in 1993 the camp had to be dismantled and all the tents and camp gear along with all the personnel, baggage and dogs were crammed into the machine for lift off. There was not an inch of spare space and we were pressed tightly together among sweating Russians and panting dogs, one of which later tried to squeeze through an open cabin window in mid-flight. Taking off seemed to be a problem and five or six times we rose a foot or two before settling back to earth. Finally we became air-born but almost immediately flew into dense fog. I was sitting just behind the pilot who indicated that he was going to try to get above the fog which he never did. We rose, I think, to about 10,000 feet and it became very cold. Umba, our destination, was about 160 miles away and looking through the windshield was like staring at blank sheet of white paper all the way. Later on I was alarmed to see the top of a fog-shrouded spruce tree flashing past the window but moments later we landed safely on Umba's helipad. The helicopter seemed to have few navigational aids and no radar.

Now and then we saw wildlife during the flights and one enthusiastic pilot pursued a herd of reindeer across the tundra banking steeply as the terrified beasts tried to out-manoeuvre us. On another occasion we located a bear which was minding its own business but which the pilot decided to chase. There did not seem to be any safety rules and when a crewman opened the door to give a better view I simply stood up and leant out of the open door, holding on with my left hand while operating a camera with my right.

In the course of twelve trips to the Kola we have been fortunate in having fished eleven different rivers. All provided good sport and a lot of fun, but two of them, the Kitsa in 2005 and the Pana in 2007, being not too large, were among the most enjoyable. The Kitsa is fast flowing and is fed from a substantial lake. In consequence its water is colder than that of the Varzuga which it joins almost at the White Sea and because of this salmon run into it a little later than into the Varzuga. It flows through spruce and birch forest and when we fished it the sun shone, turning the river cobalt blue with gleaming white breaking waves. Hemmed by the vivid green of the forest it was a pretty sight. Fishing one day with my nephew Iain, we caught twenty-five fresh-run fish between us along with a few kelts and a pike! The salmon were spread across the entire width of the river, behind almost every stone and boulder and it was pure delight to wade down, sometimes in mid-river, picking up fish on the way.

We never landed any big fish on the Kitsa, but on one occasion I had a strong take in a particularly fast run. The fish seemed exceptionally powerful and presently it turned its head downstream and raced through some rapids and just kept on going. It was impossible to follow and all my line and most of the backing were ripped off as the fish continued its unstoppable rush till it disappeared round a bend and then came off. This was certainly exciting but I think that it must have been foul hooked and was probably no bigger than others which we caught.

The Pana, a tributary of the Varzuga, must be among the best rivers on the Kola and Roxton's camp stands beside a beautiful pool at a point where another river, the Indel, joins it. The Pana is a manageable size and whereas salmon can be caught almost anywhere, it has some outstanding pools and the Pundzoi is one of the best. It lies fifteen minutes downstream from the camp by boat. Fast water runs into the long curving pool maintaining a strong current down the middle

One of the jet boats on the Pana.

until, after a hundred yards, the momentum fades into the shallows of the tail. At the neck a forest stream, from which the pool takes its name, joins the river. Wading down the left shore, starting opposite this stream, gives access to the whole pool and, when a run of fish is in, big catches are possible. Derek McIntosh and I fished there together for a morning and an afternoon and we landed 30 fish. He had one on the first cast of the day and soon afterwards I hooked one which ran for about twenty yards before coming unstuck but before I could retrieve the fly another took and was landed. All the fish were fresh-run and weighed from about 5 to 13lbs.

There are many other outstanding pools but one of the most convenient is Camp Pool at the point where the Indel joins the Pana. On one occasion Derek was fishing there watched by three allegedly off-duty Russian policemen who had appeared in camp 'for a rest'. Derek proceeded to catch five salmon in quick succession and the

The comfortable cabins at Pana Camp.

Another fish released on the Pana.

policemen, joining into the spirit of the occasion, called him a terrorist for catching so many fish. We responded by calling them the K.G.B! They turned out to be very jovial and were good company.

Transport from Pana Camp is mostly by boat but one day, for a change, we set off in an enormous, battered Russian lorry! We climbed into the cab with Tolya, the camp's mechanic, while our fishing gear and a rubber dinghy were stowed in the back along with Andrei, our guide. With the engine roaring we plunged straight across the Indel, which was by no means shallow, pushing a bow wave in front of us and emerged on the far shore with water pouring off the vehicle. This brought us to the near bank of the Pana just upstream from the junction with the Indel and from there we drove along a track of sorts which led upstream but out of sight of the river. Large boulders littered the track and now and then we ploughed on through axle-deep flooded stretches. During the journey I managed to chat to Tolya who spoke no English and on the way he told me how much better life was under

Crossing the Indel by Russian lorry; an unconventional but handy method.

112

Communist rule. He said that nowadays, if one doesn't have money, life on the Kola is very difficult and the opportunities to earn money are few and far between. Apparently Svetoslav Mikhailovich Kalyuzhen, the de facto chief administrator of the area who used to run the 'State Collective,' now operates what amounts to a welfare system so that if a guide becomes seriously ill free helicopter transport is arranged to hospital along with free treatment in Umba or Murmansk. Later on Tolya volunteered how much he hated President Bush and drew a finger across his throat when mentioning him. He was a most affable companion but was still grieving for his son who, tragically, had been drowned in the Varzuga the previous year when his boat capsized.

Svetoslav Mikhailovich Kalyuzhen (left), former chairman of the Soviet collective, and bodyguard with Kalashnikov.

After about 50 bone-shaking minutes in the lorry it was a relief to come across the Pana once more and much of the rest of the day was spent silently floating downstream in the rubber dinghy while fishing likely spots on the way until we ended up back at the camp. The main run of salmon had not then reached that part of the river but nevertheless we picked up enough fish to keep us amused while admiring the magnificent forest from the quietness of the dinghy. Although the fishing was not fast and furious there was plenty of bird life to look at including waders, terns, goosander and other ducks and in a pine tree we came across a pair of beautiful Siberian jays with orange rumps which I had never seen before.

The Pana ranks among the best rivers that I have fished and the Russian guides were among the most friendly and forthcoming. Things were a little slow during the first three days owing to high water conditions which delayed the main run but in spite of this Derek and I had about 35 fish each - he had a few more than me!

In the first week of June 2008 we again fished the Pana but spring was unusually late and the river was much too full for comfortable fishing and sinking lines with copper tube flies had to be used. The main run of fish had not entered the river when we were there and the eight rods caught just 99 salmon in six days. I actually achieved a blank day! We never tried to achieve great numbers and did not fish in the evenings preferring, instead, to enjoy a quiet vodka or two and to compare notes about the huge ones that got away.

Chapter 10

The Melancholy Magic of Grimersta

In the Outer Hebrides, defying both the Atlantic gales and the winds of social change, Grimersta Lodge clings to the shores of Loch Roag on the west coast of Lewis. Its name is inextricably linked with superlative salmon fishing in unique surroundings where often the only sounds are those of birds and the moaning of the sea wind sweeping across the headlands. For nine seasons in the 1970s and early 80s I had the privilege of staying in the lodge and fishing the Grimersta System and always, on arrival, I had a feeling of stepping back into an earlier era. The lodge is a bit like a well appointed London club but with wild and beautiful landscape at the door and, of course, with some of the finest and most varied salmon fishing in the world nearby. Whilst outside gales and rain may sweep across the landscape, inside the lodge there is a haven of Edwardian comfort - tea in the afternoons, formal dinners with fine wines and lobster for lunch on Sundays.

All of this has come about because a glacier in the last Ice Age carved out an eight mile long trench in the Lewisian gneiss which has become Loch Langavat and which feeds into the Grimersta lochs like a giant storage tank helping to maintain a steady flow of water. Oddly, two rivers flow out of Langavat into the highest of the four Grimersta lochs, all of which are interconnected with short rivers. Finally the mile long Grimersta river itself runs into the sea loch not far from the lodge.

Quite apart from the fishing the landscape alone is curiously striking with, to me, a pervasive mood of melancholy, especially in the

The Grimersta River on the Isle of Lewis.

isolation of the upper lochs. Perhaps the Norse names of some of the hills and lochs are a reminder of long dead folk who, in the end, made such little impression on the place. The people may have gone but there is plenty of wild life. Sometimes the dark speck of a soaring eagle can be seen high above the slopes of Roneval and over the lochs the occasional black-throated diver flies high and arrow-straight, cackling on its way to some distant stretch of water. Closer at hand wrens flit among the bouldered margins of the lochs and are quite unafraid of a nearby boat. It is difficult to imagine a more lonely and fascinating place in which to fish for salmon.

Catches on the system can be remarkable and in the back of my fishing album is a copy of an old 1888 photograph showing three bearded, tweed-clad ghillies holding two poles on which are draped no less than fifty-four salmon. This was a day's catch by a Mr. Naylor and is the record for the system. Nineteen eighty-two was also a

116

bumper year and one rod caught 35 fish in a day and shortly afterwards two other rods had thirty fish each. Catches like these are, of course, exceptional.

My fourth visit to Grimersta was in late August 1976, as usual, with my friend and fishing companion, David Kilpatrick. The summer had been exceptionally hot and dry but on our arrival a strong westerly wind blew up driving a heavy overcast before it. The lochs already had a good stock of fish, but enlivened by the near gale they came on the take. I have often heard it said that loch fishing for salmon must be boring, but on these waters, especially when there is a good wind, this is far from the case.

The Grimersta day starts at 9.30am. precisely with the traditional 'ghillie's march' from the far end of the lodge up to the front door to meet the 'rods'. In those days the old stagers, all of them weather-beaten Lewismen with a wealth of fishing knowledge, led the way followed by young, keen newcomers. In more recent years students from the mainland have made up the numbers as the elderly islanders have gradually passed on.

It was our good fortune to have as our ghillie Angus Macleod, an elderly Lewisman with a lovely Hebridean accent and a quiet sense of humour. Wondering if he had actually been off the island, at our first meeting David asked him if he had ever been to Edinburgh. "No," he said, "Not so far east as that, but I've been to Glasgow." Then after a long pause, "And I've been to Yokohama quite a lot." It transpired that he had been in the Merchant Navy for thirty years!

Standing in front of the lodge before setting off he checked my choice of flies, the preferred combination at that time being a black Stoat Tail on the end of the cast and a Blue Elver on a long dropper. The guinea fowl feather of this extraordinarily effective fly is sometimes up to 3 inches long and because of the very rough conditions on this first day of our visit I had selected the biggest Elver in my box. Although I have caught many salmon on the Elver at Grimersta, it is odd that I have rarely found it to be successful elsewhere.

That day, with two ghillies in the boat, we were to be on Loch Faoghail Chiorabhal, known as Loch 3 at the lodge, where the strong wind provided perfect fishing conditions. Angus rowed us over to the windward shore where substantial breakers slapped and splashed among the rocks. Rowing hard into the wind he kept the boat 20 yards off-shore and gave us his usual advice, "Fish the second wave from the shore!" The line streamed out easily in the wind that day with the Elver 'dapping' on and above the waves so that it was hardly necessary to cast. It is in these conditions that Grimersta loch fishing is so exciting, and before long we both had salmon swirling at the flies. Curiously the accepted technique is to strike as soon as a fish rises which is so unlike river fishing and if this is not done there is little chance of hooking the fish. Presently, through the side of a wave I clearly saw a salmon, jaws open, coming at my Elver which it took with a solid pull - a token strike and it was on! A good tussle followed while Angus rowed after it as best he could and in due course an 8lb fish was in the net.

Jimmy Thomson loch fishing for salmon at Grimersta.

That day David had four fish and I had two, all between 5 and 8lbs. The occasional fish lunged at the elver when it was air-born a inch or two above the waves and some were visible through the side of a wave following the fly. There could hardly be a more exciting way of hooking a salmon. Most took within a few yards of the rocks of a low lying promontory of reptilian outline appropriately named the 'Alligator', which was the real 'hot spot' of that loch. Being the first week of September the fish were becoming coloured but there was an odd fresh-run one among them. In those days few fish were returned to the water and at the end of the day the catch was tied up in polythene bags for transportation to the lodge. It used to distress me to see a bag of salmon tipped out onto the slab, slime and discolouration spoiling their beauty. After many years of fishing it gives me more pleasure to watch a released salmon swimming off than to take home a corpse.

On another day we travelled to the uppermost loch prosaically known at the lodge as Loch 4 since the beautiful Gaelic name Airigh na h-Airdie was too much for the predominantly English rods to cope with. After a quite lengthy journey involving the lodge van, two successive boat trips and some walking, we arrived at this most beautiful and isolated of all the lochs. By then it was late morning and we wasted no time in taking the boat out and headed towards the top of the loch. All around lay seemingly endless moor and scattered peat hags and although it was early September clumps of bell heather still glowed in sheltered spots around the shore. Far off beyond the head of the loch the rocky slopes of Roneval, rising to 800 feet, dominated the landscape. On its summit, over a thousand years ago, some Norseman must have stood as he surveyed this wilderness of moor and water and perhaps gave the hill its name. So inviting did the hill look that David decided to climb it for some exercise and left me in the care of Angus so that I could get on with the fishing. After about an hour and a half he returned and hailed us from the shore shouting in apparent excitement that he had found a Norse relic on the top of

The Grimersta system from the top of Roneval where a Norseman must once have stood.

Roneval, whereupon he produced a rusty, empty can of Norseman Lager which he had found in a cairn on the summit.

At the head of the loch, near the mouth of one of the Langavat rivers, is a shallow bay known as the Basin, and it was here that we began to fish. Looking down into the water anti-poacher barbed wire could be seen buoyed up with plastic bottle floats so that the whole contraption lay a foot or two beneath the surface. This made illegal netting impossible, but was a sad sign of the near state of war that has, at times, existed between a few of the locals and the fishery management. Boats have been burnt at night and there have been fights between the river watchers and poachers. When we first fished at Grimersta the fishery manager was a charming man named Roddy Livingston and he seemed to have come to a kind of rapprochement with the locals, but later a good but very tough manager was appointed and he used to patrol the sea loch in the local fishery protection launch which rejoiced in the sinister name of 'Omsk'. As well as this he often became involved in nocturnal fist-fights beside the river and lochs. One or two local poachers had it in for him and his vessel and they mounted a serious and dangerous attempt to sink the boat by dropping large boulders onto it from a bridge. Fortunately no-one was killed but the war had obviously got out of hand. In a further act of defiance the poachers burnt down a beautiful stone and timber built fishing cabin on an island in Loch Airigh na h-Airdie. Since then I believe that things have settled down perhaps with the help of less confrontational methods.

It was not difficult to put all of this out of our minds on that lovely breezy day. The Basin produced several fish in spite of the barbed wire entanglements and one or two more were taken close to the rocks of the shore nearby. Angus, watching some fish showing near the Basin, commented that those which jumped downwind were not takers, while those showing upwind were. I had not heard this before and have no idea whether the theory is true or not. In common with many of the older islanders Angus was very religious and once said that he could not ghillie for us on the following day as he had to be at 'the communions'. Rather irreverently I asked him to put a word in to the Lord on my behalf. Two days later on his return I asked if he had done as I had requested. He was silent for a minute and then replied, "Yes I did, but He was not knowing you."

One morning in the early 1980s accompanied this time by an old friend, Jimmy Thomson, we were woken in the lodge by a gale which rattled the doors and howled round the roof. The prospects for fishing seemed hopeless, but during breakfast, the wind moderated a little and along with the ghillies we set off to inspect the lochs. To our alarm one of the of the student river watchers appeared running down the loch-side in a state of exhaustion. Apparently a disaster had occurred away up in the system. Two local fishers had been heading up the Grimersta lochs to far off Loch Langavat by boat in the atrocious conditions and had been capsized by the storm and one was a non-swimmer. The student river watchers had seen this happen and, at considerable risk to themselves, had managed to bring both of the men to the shore, where at least one was said to be in a very bad way. The Grimersta fishery manager had somehow managed to get to the scene, but more help was needed. By this time the wind had again strengthened but nevertheless two ghillies prepared the heavy wooden boat for the long trip up the loch to the scene of the accident. Since I was a doctor it was thought best for me to go, but when we pushed off the reality of the storm struck home. The outboard struggled to make headway and sheets of spray swept the boat so that we had to bale hard, but for much of the time we crouched on the bottom boards with anorak hoods up and backs to the spray while waves surged past. It certainly was not safe! After about thirty minutes we made it to the scene of the accident. In the nearby fishing hut we found the manager lying under a sleeping bag trying to warm one of the men who was semiconscious from hypothermia. The other was silent and ashen in a state of hypothermic shock, but nevertheless responsive. A student and the manager smashed up all the furniture and fed it into the stove which began to roar and to give some welcome heat as everyone was soaking wet. Gradually the men revived but one remained confused and flatly refused to get into our boat for the stormy journey back down the loch. Ultimately, using a mixture of persuasion and force, both were placed aboard and sensibly someone had radioed for the Stornoway ambulance which awaited us at the loch-end.

After 24 hours in hospital the men recovered and a few days later they thoughtfully appeared at the lodge to thank us, bringing a welcome bottle of whisky! Hopefully our efforts did at least something to improve relations with the locals.

The River

Of all Highland rivers the Grimersta must be among the most attractive as it runs from the lowest loch to the sea between banks of rock and heather. The fast flow pauses in numerous pools and the odd cluster of autumn-red rowan berries hangs glowing over the water from high rocks where sheep have been unable to reach the young trees. Just below the road bridge near the sea loch is a beautiful pool which has been artificially deepened by rocks built up at the tail. In spite of its turbulent flow, on sunny days it is often possible to see glinting, silver flashes from the bottom of the pool as sea-fresh salmon try to dislodge irritating sea-lice by rubbing their itchy sides on the stones. This, the Bridge Pool, can be highly productive, but the ghillies say that when the fish act like this they rarely take.

Thirty yards downstream is the celebrated Kelt Pool. The far bank consists of a low rock cliff against which the main current flows, while on the near bank a little sheep-cropped 'lawn' projects into quiet water from which it is easy to fish the whole pool. It is said that numerous peers of the realm and sundry 'hyphenated' personages, while standing on this spot, have nicked out a quick after-dinner salmon, as it is so easily accessible from the lodge.

One evening after a fine dinner and some even finer port a certain knighted air chief marshal took his wife, who had hardly fished before, down to this hallowed spot to see if she could catch her first salmon. In due course I strolled quietly down to see what progress was being made and there she was in the act of landing a very nice salmon. Yelps of delight came from the gathering dusk and I could just see that she put the fish on a bank of peat beside the pool while she went on fishing. Silently I crept up and removed the salmon and as I fled back to the lodge in the near darkness with the slippery booty I could hear shouts of , "Oh darling, it's gone!" When she and her husband ultimately returned empty-handed saying that she really had caught a salmon but that her fish had disappeared, we all said that that was a likely story and that she was telling 'porkies'. Ultimately

I confessed to my misdeed and she received well-earned all round congratulations. Happily she was very good humoured about the affair!

To have a day on the river is a wonderful experience though, as one would expect, it fishes best when the water is settling after a spate when sport can be spectacular. I enjoy using a fairly small, light rod and on one blustery wet day when the water was running high I was lucky enough to have four fish in quick succession on a Hairy Mary and what fun they were! Some of my happiest hours have been spent working my way down this perfect little Highland river right down to where it joins the sea.

If one went to Grimersta solely to catch fish, as with all rivers and lochs, one might well be disappointed as it is quite easy to catch nothing if the water is very low or if conditions in general are not right. However, who can fail to be impressed by such magnificent surroundings? The atmosphere of the lodge in its setting, perched on the edge of the sea loch, is itself unique and, on returning from a long day's fishing, what could be better than to lie back in a hot bath with an enormous gin and tonic, listening to the sough of the Hebridean wind in the fractured trees behind the building and contemplating the events of the day?

Chapter 11

The River Thurso

Early spring fishing in Caithness can be a trial of endurance. The wind is all too often bitterly cold and sometimes sleet and snow sweep in off the grey northern sea. Salmon in the River Thurso are never numerous at that time of year but in spite of this a group of friends and I have fished there for many years during those spring months. It may well be asked why on earth we do this but the reason is that, although the fish are few and far between, they are among the most beautiful that I have caught anywhere - fat and deep bodied, gleaming silver and often quite big. Actually catching one of these rare beauties more than compensates for many blank days and I have had plenty of those. Over the years I have made thirteen visits to the Thurso involving 60 days fishing and have caught only 8 salmon - and I still love going there!

Quite apart from the salmon the landscape is curiously attractive in its own way - austere and bleak as it tilts towards the Pentland Firth under a seemingly limitless sky. It feels like the edge of the world. Not a tree interrupts the view from the single-track road which leads to Halkirk, the small village where we stay, seven miles from the town of Thurso. Bare fields are walled with upright slabs of Caithness 'slate' some etched with fossils and an occasional pallet or old bed-stead fills a gap where a slab has fallen.

Halkirk has a 'northerly look' about it, the houses huddling low on the open landscape as if hiding from the elements. The Ulbster Arms Hotel where we stay stands beside the river - so close in fact that it is possible to pop a champagne cork into the water from a bedroom window on the rare days when a salmon has actually been caught. The hotel at the time of writing is under new ownership but I hope that its slightly faded charm and the invariably warm welcome will not be lost. Opposite, the war memorial records the scores of personal tragedies suffered in this district in the two World Wars. Many good Caithness names are there - Sinclair, Forbes and many others. Halkirk is a quiet, homely place, the chimes of the town hall clock competing in the mornings with cawing from the local rookery. These and the occasional clopping of a horse's hooves are sometimes the only sounds that one hears on waking.

The river is not at all large and it is all too easy to catch your fly on the opposite bank. Its twenty-five mile course runs from Loch More in the peaty uplands and at the outflow from the loch a small dam controls water flow for the benefit of the fishing. The river then immediately runs beneath a fine arched stone bridge and continues

The bleak surroundings of upper Thurso on a cold April day in 1993.
From left: author, John Cowie and Lord Cowie.

for a few hundred yards to Loch Beag in a succession of beautiful streamy pools where salmon often lie in channels between reedy islets. This is wonderful holding water and can provide excellent sport.

Loch Beag is in a class of its own. If the salmon are there and if there is a good ripple there is a really good chance of a fish or two. It can be fished from a boat or from the bank and on one occasion I managed to wade right down the middle of the loch fishing the streamy run where the fish tend to lie. My best fish which was caught in the run-in to the loch was a fresh-run 13 pounder in 1994.

An odd thing once happened to me in the fishing hut beside this loch. It is a lonely, isolated spot miles from anywhere and one day two friends, the ghillie and I were eating our lunchtime sandwiches inside the hut when I heard clearly a woman's voice just outside the door enquiring how we were getting on. As I got to my feet I asked the ghillie if that was Lady Thurso who had arrived, but on going outside there was not a soul in sight - just open moorland for miles around. I never 'hear voices' and I had not drunk any whisky and to this day I am puzzled by that phantom voice which the others were uncertain of having heard. I have no explanation for it and at the time I found it quite disturbing.

Fishing the middle section of the river can be a bit of a penance. The river, like a lazily coiled snake, winds its way through low lying boggy land where the current is slow and I have only caught kelts there. In some parts small mud flats form the bank and on wading through these, evil smelling methane bubbles to the surface, no doubt contributing to global warming. In the cattle-trodden puddles at the water's edge I once noticed leeches oozing blackly through the mud. On cold, wet, windy days fishing there is not much fun. On one miserable sleety day two members of our party, David Ross-Stewart and Jimmy Thomson, were trudging glumly along through a riverside bog, frozen wet and fishless, when among some rushes they came across a very dead sheep. With melting sleet dripping off his cap and nose David prodded the corpse with his foot and, summing up the misery of the day, commented - "Lucky bugger !"

The lower reaches near the hotel and further downstream have plenty of attractive pools among the surrounding farmland. Fifty yards above the hotel a lane leads down to the river past a derelict stone mill-house filled with collapsing piles of hay among which comfortable hens poke about, some sitting on nests and supervised by a colourful but evil looking yellow-eyed rooster. Beside the mill is the Quarry Pool where I once had an entertaining encounter. Below a cliff on the opposite side there is a run of deep water where salmon lie and I was fishing this down when I was rewarded by a good pull. Immediately the fly was taken quickly downstream in a series of heaves. I ran down to the tail of the pool to intercept what seemed to be a good fish. Then a writhing black shape momentarily surfaced like some riverine monster and soon afterwards I successfully beached the very sporting inner tube of a bicycle tyre.

My most memorable day on the Thurso began upstream in the wild moorland part of the river which is such a joy to fish when conditions are right. It was a blustery May day in 2004 and I had walked upstream for forty minutes or so, sometimes breaking into a jog so as not to waste fishing time and came to a likely-looking though shallow pool. At the neck was a small gravel beach and from that vantage point the deeply peat stained water looked worth a try. Keeping well back and crouching down I cast an Ally Shrimp into the 'run in'. To my amazement a fish swirled at the fly though did not touch it. Cautiously I cast again and was rewarded with that wonderful 'tap' of a take and, determined to ensure that the fish was well hooked, I did nothing - until the reel began to run - and he was on! He raced around the pool several times and I admit to sending up a prayer that he would not come unstuck. The dark water made it difficult to see the fish though it seemed to be a good size and after about ten minutes it was possible to lead him up onto the beach - a beautiful fresh-run thirteen pounder complete with sea lice. What a triumph! The long trek back to the car while carrying the fish was sheer pleasure: the larks sounded even more joyful than usual and the calls of the oyster catchers and curlews over the moor seemed to celebrate as well.

After a quick bar lunch at the hotel I set off downstream to the Siulag Pools where the river forms a big 'S' bend. At the tail of the Upper Siulag the current pulls away in a beautiful deep glide over clean gravel and it was here that, almost unbelievably, another fish took. Once again it seemed to be powerful and took my fly two hundred yards downstream while I ran to keep up. In due course it came to the bank where I struggled, netless, to tail it but finally lifted out a perfect 17lb. fresh run fish.

Behind the Ulbster Arms Hotel, Halkirk, with the 17lb springer from the Siulag Pool. A particularly beautiful specimen. April 2004.

What a day it had been, for me at that time of year on the Thurso; quite exceptional. The first fish ultimately formed the centrepiece of a buffet lunch at my brother's 70th. birthday party and how delicious it was.

In early May 2006 an old school friend, Rowland Robinson , and I went up to the Thurso for three days even though the weather was unfavourable, with several days of unbroken sunshine. The water level was on the low side and we fished for the first two days without even seeing a fish but the sunlit views over to Orkney helped to make up for the lack of activity. On the last day we were on beat nine, the moorland stretch, which I so enjoy and, having seen no signs of salmon, I came to the Rock Pool. The water was low and in the bright conditions prospects seemed hopeless. On the far side a big patch of white foam lay at the edge of the current, and above it the

Two well known Thurso gillies – the late Morris Murray (left) and Jim MacDonald

bank was aflame with yellow gorse. Standing well back I cast the usual Ally Shrimp into the foam and the current, taking a belly of line, swung the fly nicely across the pool. To my great surprise a fish took with a powerful bang and raced up and down the quite small pool. I was using a little 9 foot rod and never really gained control and sadly, after five or six minutes, the fly pulled out. To lose a rare Thurso springer is a disaster and I am sorry to say that my language reflected the fact. Like all my lost fish it was, of course, a really big one! An hour and a half later I returned to the same spot to try again in the hope that more than one fish was there. On stepping cautiously into the shallows a dark underwater shape swam off not four feet from me, trailing a stream of bubbles. For a moment I wondered if it could be my salmon in a bad way after having been hooked, but bubbles? Impossible. Then a head poked out of the water - an otter! It seemed useless to continue and I packed up for the day. However, in retrospect, it seems possible that the otter had been around for some time and had perhaps disturbed the pool and the fish which had taken my fly was settling back into, and was defending, its lie. Most of us have heard stories of ghillies stoning a pool or even sending in a dog to unsettle fish in the belief that they might then be more inclined to take once back in their lies. Perhaps an otter in the vicinity has the same effect - who knows?

There are many more lovely pools on the Thurso but one, the Mill Stream, deserves special mention. A few hundred yards below the Rock Pool the river runs beneath a narrow road and, soon after emerging, an outcrop of layered rock narrows the flow which cascades into the most perfect pool below. On the high ground of the opposite bank a venerable, disused stone mill-house overlooks the water, its window openings staring blindly over the Caithness landscape. The pool is easy to fish from a shoulder-high rock platform beside the falls and from that vantage point I was once lucky enough to hook a fish. A scrabbling clamber off the platform ensued with the rod held aloft in one hand while the salmon performed its antics in the pool below.

I never seem to have a net handy but nevertheless managed to beach another good Thurso fish this time of 10 lbs.

Although spring salmon may not be numerous in the Thurso there are many compensations. In such a small community everyone is very friendly - where else can one expect a cheery toot and a wave from the train driver as he passes a fisherman at a pool? At that time of year nature is beginning to emerge from its winter torpor and along the lower reaches of the river steep banks are lit with clusters of pale primroses and the world is filled with the calls of moorland birds - larks, lapwings, curlews and oyster catchers. One day an osprey paid us a visit while we were fishing. Once, on a dry bank, we surprised an adder basking in the April sunshine. The ghillies wanted to kill it but instead I gently prodded it with my rod butt which it struck leaving a spot of moisture on the rubber as it slid away into the dead bracken. Otters are quite common and on one occasion I came upon a pair playing among some gorse bushes beside the river not ten yards from me. The Caithness landscape may be austere and stark and the spring weather can be bracing but there is a wealth of bird and animal life - and with just the occasional salmon too!

Chapter 12

The River Naver

Perhaps I should have been warned by the deer on the journey north. Hundreds of them had come off the Sutherland hills and were foraging beside the road in Strath Vagastie near Althaharra, rather undernourished looking beasts, few heavier than about twelve stones and with thin horn. Above them the dark, snow dusted hulk of Ben Klibrek had an odd air of menace as hail squalls lashed across the low ground. A storm from the north was on its way.

A group of friends and I planned to stay at Skelpick Lodge and to fish the River Naver for three days in late March 2007 with just a chance of catching one of its beautiful springers. Northerly gales are tiresome at the best of times, but this was a really bad one which did not bode well for the fishing. After arriving we went on a few miles to Bettyhill on the north coast to have a look at the river mouth. Far out to sea ranks of huge waves, driven by the on-shore north wind, built higher and higher with spray ripping off their curling tops before collapsing in a roaring maelstrom of white foam which filled much of the bay. Further off, at the foot of some low cliffs, great plumes of spray rose majestically skywards. To make matters worse squalls of hail and snow promised to make fishing an ordeal - which it was! All that night the lodge was rocked by the gale. Hail rattled at the windows as though shards of glass, flying through the darkness, were striking the panes.

Usually the Naver is a lovely river but on our first day its character was washed out by a water level four feet above normal and many of the pools were unfishable. Even standing in the wind was an effort, while casting and keeping the line in the water was a struggle. Not surprisingly none of us had any luck.

On the following day the wind had moderated slightly and the river level had fallen a foot. I was to fish the Island Stream a short distance below the lodge but access to its potentially holding water was a problem. The top of the bank was lined with gorse and fishing

Col. Bill Bewsher, one of our party, enduring a foul, snowy day on the Naver in March 2007.

from behind this spiny barrier made it difficult to hold a fly over possible lies. The alternative was to climb down into chest deep water to cover the 'draw' at the edge of the current. With some trepidation I decided to try this and, using a sinking line with a two inch Comet dressed on a copper tube, worked my way steadily down the pool. At about eleven in the morning, during a particularly foul shower of hail, my fly had swung to directly below me when a fish took. It was not the sort of take when one has time to pause or to give line, but with a wallop the fish made off on a mighty run out into the fast water. I was worried that it might be lightly hooked as it had taken 'on the dangle' but it stayed on. When a fish takes in spring there is always the chance that it is a kelt, but there was no doubt about this one. It stayed far out in the heavy current and only after ten minutes did it come into the quieter water near me: then the problem arose of where to land it. Euan, the ghillie, was far away with one of the other rods and, as usual, I had no net and could not get ashore owing to the gorse thicket hanging over the water. However, coaxing the fish downstream for fifty yards brought me to a small sandy beach where it was possible to draw it up onto the sand. It was a lovely deep bodied springer of about twelve pounds and was hooked well down in the mouth - a really secure hold. On gently returning it to the water it swam off seemingly none the worse for wear.

On the third day the wind had moderated though it was still cold with intermittent snow squalls and Euan took me to try the upper beat not far below Loch Naver. The single-track road to the beat passes several recently erected memorials to communities evicted in the Highland Clearances and to this day there is a palpable feeling of an emptied landscape. The remains of moss covered walls on the hillsides mark the spots where the once thriving communities existed.

My good fortune of the previous day was not repeated but I enjoyed the wildness of the countryside. Although there were few signs of spring, a skein of greylag geese passed overhead on the way

Old ruins on the banks of Loch Naver resulting from the Highland Clearances of the early 19th Century.

Highland Clearance monument at the site of Rossal by Loch Naver.

north, possibly to Iceland and one or two pairs of stubby-bodied goldeneye duck flew along the river. At one pool we disturbed a depressed looking heron which flapped off into the wind like an old grey dish towel. I was evidently not the only fisher on the river that day and beside another pool we came upon an otter's 'scat', the black droppings filled with fish bones and one or two bright silver scales which, I hoped, were from kelts.

By the time we left the river the level was falling steadily, exposing the bare winter twigs of riverside bog myrtle. The weather had moderated and although Ben Klibrek still loomed beyond Loch Naver it no longer looked menacing and there was just a hint of spring in the air. I departed in the happy knowledge that I would be back on the river in July.

July. Summer Grilse.

It was difficult to believe that this was the same river that we had fished only four months previously. It was as if there had never been any wind and hail and the moor below Loch Naver was alive with summer growth. Riverside banks of bog myrtle scented the air and yellow candles of bog asphodel lit the sombre moor while clusters of pink spotted orchids imparted a pleasantly frilly feminine touch.

The river was in excellent condition: the grilse were said to be up and fishing prospects looked good for our six day visit. Even the weather was perfect - cool and showery with blinks of sunshine and so different from the wintry storm of our previous visit. At the top of the beat, just below the loch, a tributary, the Mallart, joins the River Naver in a cascading welter of white water and 150 yards below this Bob McBain, the head keeper, started me off in one of his favourite spots. One or two silver flashes of moving grilse showed in the shallow, fast-streaming runs between shelves of rock but there was no pool in the traditional sense of the word. I had decided to use a little nine foot rod with a small Silver Stoat and began by fishing a smoothly running channel which looked a little deeper than the rest. After only

Releasing a tagged summer grilse on the Naver.

a few casts a fish splashed at the fly but without connecting. It came again no less than four more times and then Bob changed the fly for the smallest Black Stoat in my box. Sure enough this did the trick and at once the game little grilse began cavorting among the rock channels, bending the small rod and giving a great fight. After a few minutes the most perfect little fish of 4 or 5 lbs. and carrying sea lice came to the net and was duly tagged and returned. I had always been under the impression that sea lice drop off salmon after 48 hours in fresh water but, apparently, on the Naver tagged fish have been re-caught after five days still carrying the parasites.

This set the pattern for the rest of the week and for four rods we had thirty grilse one of which was caught by the cook from our lodge. All were 'sea fresh' except one which had probably been in the river for two or three weeks and which had actually taken an Elver fly.

Summer grilse fishing is such a joy and is so different from the 'chuck and chance it' approach which may be necessary in early spring. The fish often lie in fast water behind quite small rocks and stones, sometimes close to the bank beneath overhanging branches and little side casts with a small rod may be the only way of reaching them. Bob McBain was an excellent adviser and was adamant that casts should be made well downstream in order to prevent a belly of line from preceding the fly over the fish and he advocated fast stripping in of the line over the lies. The flies which he preferred were all small and these certainly seemed to be effective though to my surprise he once suggested trying a sizeable Elver on the dropper which promptly caught the fish mentioned above.

The Naver is a lovely river in both spring and summer and as this fishing season draws to a close I look forward to going back next spring, in spite of likely snow or floods!

A tranquil stretch of the Naver.

Bob McBain, head keeper, indicating a lie on the upper Naver

Chapter 13

East Greenland

After many years of fishing together David Kilpatrick and I have begun to enjoy reconnoitering trips to places where we have never fished but rather wish that we had. During the summer of 2006 we went to look at the rivers of East Iceland and stayed at an isolated farm which looks out over a thousand miles of sea towards Norway's North Cape. We happened to wander down to the shore and came across a young man working beside a shed. On approaching him we were surprised to see that he was dark skinned with oriental eyes - certainly very different from the average Icelander - and I took him to be from the Far East. However, later on, our Icelandic landlady explained that he was, in fact, an Inuit from Greenland on a work experience visit and it was this chance meeting that made us think about investigating the fishing possibilities there.

We had heard that only one river in Greenland, the Kapisigdlit in the south-west, has a small run of salmon but the arctic char is the main migratory species and fishing for it has become quite well established in the rivers of that region. However in the end we decided that the sparsely populated east coast of Greenland might be more interesting than the more developed south-west, even though the east coast rivers are small.

That evening in the Icelandic farmhouse with the help of a little vodka we planned a 'recce trip' to the isolated Inuit settlements of Kulusuk and Angmagssalik on Greenland's east coast. Actual fishing was not to be a priority but we would take a rod just in case!

So it was that the following summer we found ourselves on a flight in a Fokker turboprop aircraft from Iceland to Kulusuk, one of many islands which make up the Greenland coast. After a short stay there we planned to fly by helicopter to Angmagssalik, also known as Tassilaq, a neighbouring island, where there is a larger Inuit settlement with the additional attraction of a small river.

After nearly two hours of flying time Greenland's black snow-streaked mountains came into view and far below us on the sea pack-ice began to thicken while enormous icebergs, like broody hens, jostled amongst the floes. Kulusuk, where we landed, has a gravel air strip which was built by the Americans in the Cold War and which

Ice off the East Greenland coast.

142

A roadside cemetery near Kulusuk.

used to service a Distant Early Warning station on the island. A blast of refrigerated air greeted us when the aircraft doors were opened, a reminder that Greenland's ice-cap was only 25 miles away and on the nearby fjord there were brilliant white ice-floes, shading to turquoise and aquamarine beneath the surface of the sea.

We checked in to the excellent small hotel near the airstrip and then took a half hour walk on a rough track to the Inuit settlement. Apparently an Inuit woman was killed by a polar bear on this track some years ago and there were certainly bears about as a few days after we arrived one was shot on the ice near Kulusuk. However, the only wild animal we met was a hungry-looking arctic fox outside my hotel window! In the thin soil beside the track scattered graves were marked with crosses and outside a wooden house an Inuit hunter was skinning three seals while his chained sledge dogs watched in slavering silence.

Later an Inuit who, a day or two later shot the polar bear, took us by boat across the fjord to a glacier on the far coast. A small rocky island off the end of the glacier evidently served as a kind of canine Alcatraz. In summer a pack of howling sledge dogs is marooned there and is fed by meat or fish occasionally thrown from a boat onto the rocks. As the climate has warmed during the last decade or so other islets have appeared from under the ice as the glacier has gradually receded. Our time at Kulusuk was short but we arranged to be driven up to the abandoned and now demolished, American early warning radar station on a high point of the island. All the buildings have gone but the concrete foundations remain - a monument to the Cold War - overlooking a remarkable blue and white view of sea, floes and icebergs.

The helicopter ride to Angmagssalik takes only about ten minutes across an ice-strewn fjord and over - only just over, it seemed - a rocky ridge near the landing ground. Not far off small, brightly painted wooden houses of the settlement crowd the slopes which lead down to the harbour where one or two boats were moored and a tiny river races beneath the road and into the harbour. The river really is small but nevertheless three Inuit boys were fishing at the mouth with small spoons and one was carrying a pair of arctic char on a string. I never fail to admire the beauty of these fish which David and I have caught in numerous countries including Iceland, Baffin Island in the Canadian Arctic, Finnmark in Norway, Newfoundland and Alaska. In 1977, near David's home in Argyll, a boy caught a one-and-a-half pound landlocked char, a genetic relic of migratory ancestors which must have teemed in the glacial rivers of Europe during the last Ice Age.

It turned out that, rightly so, the fishing on this tiny Greenland river is reserved for the Inuit population, therefore we decided to explore the river upstream towards where it emerges from the

Angmagssalik.

mountains. A scattering of wooden houses, many with tethered sledge dogs outside, were soon left behind and we found ourselves in a delightful valley known locally as The Valley of Flowers with the river rushing among rocks beside us. Around the river grew a profusion of dwarf arctic willow, an inch or two in height, and yellow flowers gleamed on the grassy slopes, while far ahead a blaze of sunlit snowfields shone on the mountains.

After a quarter of a mile, over a rise in the valley floor, we came across a graveyard, an acre of ground covered with un-inscribed wooden crosses, most of them draped with bright plastic flowers or

Inuit boys with migratory arctic char from a stream running through the Valley of Flowers.

A Scottish 1½ lb landlocked char from Loch Seil in Argyll. Caught by a boy in 1977.

*An arctic char stream in the Valley of Flowers near Angmagssalik,
East Greenland.*

pieces of coloured ribbon all fluttering gently in the light breeze. It did not seem in the least a melancholy place in such beautiful surroundings. Further upstream the little river emerged from a blue lake before continuing on its way past us down cascades and pools and on through the valley below.

The following day I walked further up the river and then branched off to scramble up a 3000ft mountain which overlooks the Valley of Flowers and Angmagssalik. On my way up a flock of snow buntings flew off, but there was not a sound of birds or wind or water. Climbing on the crumbling, frost-blasted rock was not altogether safe and the approach to the summit had to be negotiated on all fours. However, the view from the top made up for it. Out to sea the pack-ice had thickened and more stately icebergs had come into view, whilst inland a seemingly endless progression of mountain peaks and snowfields swooped and soared towards Greenland's ice cap.

Later, down in a valley, I came across a big lake where arctic char were playing in the sandy shallows, their white-edged fins clearly visible in the sunshine and I wished that I had had my rod with me! However it was a good walk and more than five hours passed before I arrived back in Angmagssalik exhilarated by the exercise, the beauty of the little river and the splendour of the mountains.

Nearly fifty years previously David and I had accompanied an Inuit hunter into the pack-ice of Frobisher Bay off Baffin Island in Canada. The considerable privations and risks of that hunting trip are still imprinted on our minds - the constant cold in the open canoe, miserable nights marooned on ice-bound beaches or tied to drifting floes, the diet of seal meat and the wolves. This time we decided to do things in comfort and arranged to go out in a converted fishing boat. When we emerged from the fjord we found that ice had blocked access to the open sea. Ahead lay a barrier of crowded floes with enormous icebergs towering above them, some angular with sheer cliffs of ice plunging 300 feet to the sea and others with glassy valleys

Icebergs in the feeding grounds of Greenland's arctic char.

and ridges riven with cracks and splits. We were looking at ancient ice. The birth of these blue and white monsters was not so much the time when they had broken away from some glacier, but rather many thousands of years ago when they were laid down in the howling darkness of prehistoric snowstorms raging across the ice-cap.

That icy seascape looked so pure and innocent but we were told that the sea food chain contains pollutants brought by currents from industrialised countries which allegedly cause higher than expected levels of cancer among the Inuit who eat so much fish and seal meat. Many also blame the present global warming on human activity and point to contrails of transatlantic airliners criss-crossing the Greenland sky.

Our time in Greenland - barely a week - gave little opportunity to meet the local people. However, on Sunday we attended a church service conducted in the Inuit language. The parka-like hood of the minister's black vestments seemed to hint at his hunting heritage. The hymn book was in phonetic Inuit and although we understood nothing, it was easy to enjoy the singing and to follow a baptism which took place at the end of the service, the mother in a magnificent beadwork collar and both proud parents in their best patterned sealskin boots kneeling at the altar on sealskin cushions.

All too soon it was time to leave Greenland. We had hardly had time to feel the heartbeat of that vast place though perhaps we did a little better than some day tourists who, having spent an hour or two there, were on our return flight to Iceland and were presented with ornate certificates confirming that they had 'been to Greenland'.

Clearly the char fishing potential in the areas which we visited was minimal, but looking into the possibilities gave us a great excuse to glimpse a marvellous part of the world - the beauty of the little river in its Valley of Flowers, the huge views of the encircling mountains and the ice-choked sea.

Arctic flowers

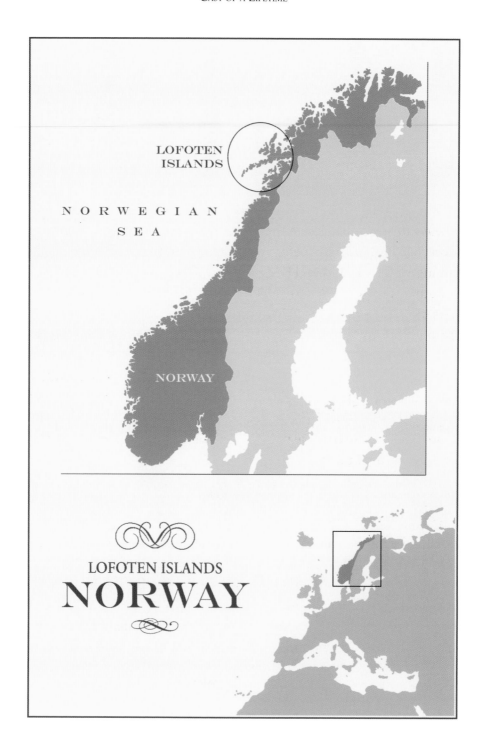

LOFOTEN
ISLANDS

N O R W E G I A N
S E A

NORWAY

LOFOTEN ISLANDS
NORWAY

Chapter 14

The Lofotens

Scouting unfamiliar territory for possible salmon fishing is always fun but this pioneering sense of search and discovery is lost if everything is arranged beforehand by a fishing agent. So it was that in August 2007 David and I decided to investigate the Lofoten Islands in rather the same spirit as we did when we were youngsters - which was quite a long time ago! Forty-nine years previously, in 1959, when on our way to look for fishing in North Norway, we had travelled through this cluster of islands which lie off the Norwegian coast, 150 miles north of the Arctic Circle. At that time their stupendous mountains and fjords caught our imagination and, on this occasion, we hoped to find out if there were any salmon rivers and at the same time to see as much of the place as possible. The inevitable fly rod lay at the bottom of my baggage.

Svolvaer, the capital, was our initial destination. Sixty-six years earlier in 1941 it had also been the destination of No3 and No4 Commando who raided the German occupied islands. They destroyed a fish oil factory which had been producing ingredients used in the manufacture of explosives, eleven ships and captured two hundred and sixteen enemy soldiers. Now the small town, backed by a mass of rocky mountains, is peaceful but memories of its foreign occupation persist and in the centre of town is a war museum containing extensive memorabilia of those years.

We spent the first night in a dock-side hotel through the open windows of which drifted the aroma of fish from the harbour. No-one knew of any salmon fishing in the vicinity and in the morning we

The Lofoten Islands have numerous 'rivers' which are really channels emptying inland extensions of fjords when the tide falls.

hired a car to drive to the extreme south-western tip of the islands past farms and fjords and mountains. Once the road crossed a small bridge over what appeared to be a superb little river rushing down through rocks to the fjord. However, closer inspection revealed that the thirty yard long 'river' was in fact a channel emptying an inland extension of the fjord as the tide fell. We continued to the end of the road at a settlement oddly named 'Å' but there were no significant rivers worth investigating. The landscape, however, was magnificent and we spent two nights in Henningsvaer, a picturesque little island settlement reached by a bridge. The hotel on its wooden piles leans over the harbour and the sound of the sea wind punctuated by the chug of departing fishing boats and squawk of gulls drifted pleasantly through my open window.

During our journey towards the northern part of the islands the fine weather broke and cloud descended on the mountain tops. Now and then shafts of sunlight pierced the overcast glinting on waterfalls pouring down dark rock faces. Once when we waited for a ferry a sea eagle planed effortlessly on the up-draughts above us. On two occasions the road crossed what seemed to be substantial rivers surging beneath bridges to the nearby fjords but, as before, these again turned out to be salt water channels emptying inland extensions of the fjords as the tide fell. The journey north was broken at Sortland, a rather undistinguished port, but there we heard that salmon did indeed exist in a little river system further north at Buknesfjord.

The Buksnesvassdragt System supports a healthy run of salmon and, apparently, increasing numbers of sea trout.

Having spent two nights in Sortland we headed north to find the river and stopped at a timber house with grass growing on the roof and which advertised meals. It was run by a Norwegian lady and her British husband who, as a Marine, had fought in the Falklands. They pointed out the river a few hundred yards further on and provided us with a good light lunch and much helpful information. The river system with its chain of lakes is called the Buksnesvassdragt and about 400 salmon are caught annually, mostly on the fly. The fish are sometimes quite big - up to 18 lbs. Many sea trout, which have become much more numerous in recent years, are also taken along with a few migratory arctic char. To fish the system a National Permit and a Local Permit have to be bought, the former costing about £20 and the latter about half as much. Our host maintains a bag net off the mouth of the river and catches around 20 salmon annually. He took us in his boat out onto the fjord to check the net but apart from some mauve and other huge brown jellyfish it was empty.

Berries beside the river, unfortunately inedible.

A Lofoten fjord with a tide-induced 'river'.

The Lofoten coastline near Svolvaer.

We walked down the road to where a small bridge spans a pair of channels which drain a substantial and apparently brackish lake on the upstream side and which then flow into the fjord on the other side of the bridge. At first the lake surface was undisturbed but then several silver grilse jumped and clearly a good stock of fish was in. Our subsequent explorations further upstream revealed a chain of other lakes joined by a tiny rivers amongst thick birch scrub. It was a most attractive spot backed by distant mountains and on the tussocky ground grew clusters of bright red berries which looked good to eat but turned out to be pithy and inedible. Sadly our time schedule did not allow us to fish but if we had done so success might well have rewarded our efforts. At least we had seen our first Lofoten salmon.

We returned by ship to Svolvaer through some of the most dramatic fjord and mountain scenery imaginable and, on approaching the harbour, the evening sun emerged and lit the encircling mountains in a spectacular farewell to these fascinating islands.

Chapter 15

Last Casts into Years Gone By

Spey Days

There have been too many marvellous fishing times to mention them all but certain other rivers have been very special over the years. The Spey in particular was my happy hunting ground when I was a medical student and in my early years as a young doctor.

In those days a friend and I used to stay at the Craigellachie Hotel as it had the fishing on the right bank of the Spey from near Aberlour right down to Craigellachie rail bridge. We often had the beat to ourselves in spring and the Tunnel Pool, the Slabs and the Bridge Pool could all be quite productive. The Bridge Pool in particular is an attractive spot. A stony beach pushes the current against a high cliff on the opposite side where pine trees cling to the near vertical slope. The pool widens as it flows beneath the beautiful Telford bridge which used to carry the road to Rothes. Thirty yards above the arch of the bridge at the foot of the cliff is a little eddy called the Doo's Nest where I once, with a trout rod and an old fashioned greased line, took an 8lb. salmon on a fly floating on the surface.

We fished other beats as well and our favourites were Wester Elchies and Upper Kinermony near Aberlour. We were rather impecunious but by befriending the ghillies in the pub we were allowed the odd day's fishing if we handed in any fish that we caught. In the summer months we sometimes started fishing after the regular rods packed up at 5pm. giving us some of the best hours of the day. However, this unofficial arrangement once got me into an awkward spot.

It was in the cold March of 1962 when almost no fish were being caught on any of the nearby beats. Prospects looked bleak. In those days I often fished a spinner in early spring and one day I put on a home made devon minnow. It was one of my favourite baits which I had made from the piece of wood through which the wire of a bucket handle passes. I had shaped it up with a chisel, fitted it with plastic fins and had painted it brown and yellow. A swivel, some copper tubing, an inch of wire inside and a treble hook made it as serviceable as anything produced by Hardy.

That afternoon I began fishing with this minnow in a pool with the beautiful Gaelic name of Pol mo Chridh' or Pool of my Heart. Without feeling very hopeful I had fished steadily half way down when something big took. It stayed out in the main current at first and then seemed determined to run down through some very fast water to the pool below. With a bit of effort it was coaxed back upstream at which point I realized that I had company. The local gravedigger had been wandering along the river and was startled to find someone playing what seemed to be a big fish at a time when almost no fish were being caught anywhere. He watched while I tailed a beautiful 22lb. fresh run springer, complete with sea lice. This was my biggest fish to date and I was quite excited about it. Clearly, however, it would not be long before the news spread far and wide. We caught nothing else that afternoon and in due course handed in the salmon at the ghillie's house rather suspecting that it would be he and not the proprietor who would benefit financially from its sale.

Two weeks after having returned home I received a letter from the owner of the beat, who had obtained my address through the hotel at which we had been staying, saying that he had heard that I had caught a big salmon when fishing unofficially on his beat. Apparently the ghillie was denying that such a fish had been caught and would I please confirm that I had, indeed, landed the fish. This put me in an awkward position as I felt some loyalty to the ghillie, so I telephoned him asking what on earth I should do. He was adamant that I should back his story saying that I knew nothing about such a fish, but as this would have involved telling an outright lie I was unwilling to agree. In the end I wrote back to the owner saying that, in the circumstances, I felt unable to make any comment.

If the story had ended there I might have emerged without too much loss of honour but with the brass neck of youth I had the cheek to write again to the owner a few months later asking permission to fish his beat. The beginning of the reply was couched in the most courteous terms but on turning the page he continued, with complete justification - "However, I was exceedingly surprised to receive your letter and you may certainly not fish my water." It is said that it is bad luck to meet a grave digger and, on this occasion, it probably was - for the ghillie.

We had many other happy days on the Spey one of which I especially remember because of the fly which I was using which I had called 'The Hairy Wife.' It was a rather fine looking home-made specimen with a bunch of my wife's then dark hair tied on a double hook. Like me many years before, a salmon fell for it. I was standing in the middle of some rapids when a good fish behind a boulder took the offering and promptly shot off downstream. It took me some time to catch up but before too long I managed to beach a fresh 15 lb. beauty.

Night fishing for sea trout on the Spey used to be thrilling sport and it never ceased to amaze me how the fish were often in water of little more than ankle depth. They were good fish too, weighing up to 5lb. The only other place where I have had such fine sea trout fishing is Loch Eilt near Arisaig where I once had a fish of over 8 lbs. but those were the days before salmon cages near the mouth of the River Ailort ruined the famous Eilt fishery. However, my biggest sea trout ever was from the Tweed and weighed 10lbs.

During our visits to the Spey we usually called in to Munro's tackle shop in Aberlour. One day in the shop I noticed a fine old Hardy 'Perfect' reel for sale at the very low price of £5 and a pair of

A 10lb sea trout from Dryburgh beat on the Tweed. June 1996.

*Comparison between the 10lb sea trout (top) and a 9lb grilse caught on the
same day.*

nearly new chest length waders for £3. When I asked why the prices were so reasonable we were told - "Ah well you see, they are being sold for the widow of a ghillie who drowned in a deep pool not so long ago. He was wearing these waders at the time." I bought the reel but did not fancy the waders!

The Awe

I can remember the Awe in the 1950s when it used to flow in untamed magnificence before the hydroelectric dam controlled the flow forever. It surged along the Pass of Brander on its way to Loch Etive and, as a boy, I used to cast longing eyes at it when the family drove north for our annual holiday at Arisaig. It is still a superb river with wonderful scenery around it and the salmon stocks seem to be reasonably healthy. I have been lucky enough to have fished it over many years, always in the hope of catching one of its famous monsters but my best so far is a 16lb. fish taken on the last cast of a day. However, I once witnessed what was probably a very big fish being played and lost in the Barrage Pool just below the dam.

That day I was fishing on the left bank of the pool and a young teenage boy was fishing opposite me. A sudden shout indicated that he had a fish on whereupon his father came running to give advice. For a long time the fish cruised about in the huge pool never showing itself. This went on for no less than two hours when suddenly the rod straightened and the fish was gone. Apparently the fly line had become detached at the junction with the backing and the fish was somewhere in the pool towing thirty yards of line. About three hours later I noticed a fly line six yards out from my bank which I managed to hook with my own fly and gently pulled at it by hand. There was no doubt about it - the fish was still on! With a good deal of manoeuvring the line was returned to its rightful owner and was re-attached to the backing. The fight immediately resumed and the fish continued to cruise about as before in spite of obvious considerable pressure being applied and it never once showed itself. This went on for another two hours at which point the hook finally pulled out. I can imagine what that young fisher must have felt!

It was on the Awe that I was reminded of the importance of giving a taking fish plenty of time before tightening. One autumn I was on an attractive pool known as Woodrow's in the wooded part of the river. The trees were changing to gold and a cluster of Monbretia, having escaped from someone's garden, glowed orange in the dimness of the woods. It was a lovely autumn, though the fish, too, were becoming coloured. At the neck of the pool a fish took and I gave it what I thought was a reasonable time before tightening - and he was gone! Ten minutes later I had another touch and this time gave a good loop of line before tightening. It turned out to be an 8lb. fish hooked in the tip of its upper jaw, a really tenuous hold. At the tail of the pool I had a third take and this time I decided to do nothing. After a few minutes a salmon started jumping about in the pool with my line clearly visible trailing behind it. It was a coloured fish of 5lbs. well and truly hooked deep in the 'scissors', a hold which would never have torn out.

Spates in the Outer Hebrides

In summer a sudden rise in the water level in the small burns and rivers of the Outer Hebrides is often accompanied a good run of sea trout or salmon which may take freely. The smallest burn where I have seen this happen is on Harris. Many years ago my wife and I were staying there in a cottage with our great friend Jimmy Thomson, his wife Margaret and their three young sons. Jimmy was a surgeon who loved fishing but he also loved surgery because, he said, it is the only blood sport with no closed season. He had a great zest for most things in life and had transmitted his enthusiasm for fishing to his sons.

The cottage was attractively situated beside a sea loch with views across the Minch to Skye and nearby a tiny burn trickled down the hillside, passed under the road and went on into the sea. The weather had been hot and dry and the hillsides were parched, but then one evening the heavens opened. The deluge assumed almost biblical proportions. The surface of the sea loch became covered with a mist of silver spray as huge raindrops hammered into it and the hills streamed with water. It rained for most of the night and we slept to the sound of gurgling gutters and drainpipes and in the morning went for a wet walk to look at the burn.

We opened the cottage door to the sound of rushing water from the burn which had been transformed into a torrent. To my surprise sea trout were showing here and there as they forged their way up this hitherto tiny stream. We hurried back to the cottage to dig for worms and returned with Niall, the youngest boy, who had never caught a fish of any size in his life. He set up his rod and dropped a worm into the racing water and almost at once it was taken by a sea trout. The fish charged off downstream and, as the youngster could not keep up over the rough ground, I lifted him by the back of his jersey and we gave chase. Having caught up we were able to slide it out of the water onto the sodden grass of the bank. It was a lovely 1lb. sea trout. In the next forty minutes Niall caught half a dozen similar fish and then the run was over and it was as if the sea trout had never been there.

A flush of new water after a dry spell, even if induced artificially, sometimes produces similar superb fishing conditions. On an earlier occasion some friends and I spent a week on the Blackwater near Callanish on the Isle of Lewis. The estate, Garynahine, was then owned by long standing friends, Willie and Frank Thyne. There had been no rain for several weeks and the salmon were still in the sea loch waiting for a spate and no-one had caught anything. On the second last day the three rods assigned to fish upstream set off planning to meet with the downstream party at lunch time. At the appointed hour they came back downriver to the sea pool to find those fishing there brimming with enthusiasm. They explained that a shoal of some kind of sea fish had entered the pool and would take avidly any small fly that had silver in the dressing and as well as this they were great fun to catch. There, in a basket, lay about a dozen beautiful fish which looked rather like whiting.

After a hurried lunch the two parties changed round and those who had been flogging the empty upper reaches settled in on the sea pool with trout fly rods and little silver flies. All afternoon they fished and fished without a touch of any kind. Disconsolately they returned to the lodge late in the afternoon to find the others, who had not bothered fishing any more, enjoying rather a lot of whisky. The disappointed fishers were only slightly amused to learn that the whiting had, in fact, been bought at the fishmonger's in Stornoway early that morning!

The point of this story, however, is to show just how rewarding it can be to fish for salmon after a long awaited rise in the water level. Most of the lodge party, who had taken such a generous amount of whisky after the whiting episode, had headaches and got up very late next day, but our hosts had arranged for an artificial spate in the night by opening the sluices on a dammed loch upstream. By morning the river had developed a minor spate and Willie and I started fishing early, not far from the lodge. It was soon apparent that salmon had poured into the river overnight and that they were in, what amounted to, a taking frenzy. Sometimes it was not even necessary to cast the fly but simply drawing it through the water resulted in bow waves of, sometimes, more than one fish charging at the fly. I have never before seen salmon competing so furiously in this way and after three hours we had ten fish between us. What a marvellous end that made to an otherwise fishless week and a reminder not to lie in bed when an overnight spate has occurred!

Finale.

It seems appropriate to end this book by looking forward with hope to the future. It all began for me sixty-six years ago when, as a boy, I peered over the parapet of an old stone bridge near Moffat and saw my first salmon. I was reminded of this the other day when I stood on a rather similar bridge in Peeblesshire, just outside my front gate, watching Tweed salmon spawning in the Lyne Water below me with a particularly aggressive cock fish lunging repeatedly at competitors. No doubt hundreds of eggs now lie buried securely in the gravel. The weakened spawning fish have since been washed away by floods but in spring the eggs will hatch and the cycle will start all over again. I hope that other young fishers will have as much fun as I have had pursuing, admiring and respecting new generations of this marvellous fish.

Index